Uncle Gary's
Business Foundations:
A Beginner's Guide to Personal Preparedness

Gary D. Urban

www.upiurbanpartners.com

Copyright © 2021 Gary D. Urban

All rights reserved.

Contents

Introduction 4
Background 6
Conversation 1 – Embrace Goals 13
Conversation 2 – Decide and Move 23
Conversation 3 – Know the Safe Exits 32
Conversation 4 - Listening 42
Conversation 5 – It Isn't Personal and You're Going to Need a Cold Heart 56
Conversation 6 – Use Your Experts 69
Conversation 7 – Ask and Ye Shall Receive 74
Conversation 8 – Dealing With Naysayers 81
Conversation 9 – Trust Yourself 85
Conversation 10 – Communicate 101
Conversation 11 - Lead 109
Conversation 12 – Form Alliances 120
Conversation 13 – It's In the Contract 126
Conversation 14 – Expect Change 132
Conversation 15 – Useful Hints 142
Epilogue 146
About the Author 147

Introduction

Another book on business, just what the world needed, right? Well, I think you'll find this one a little different. First, it's short, not filled with unnecessary jargon or complicated charts and process flows. Second, it's written to be a practical guide to key principles to help you in your day-to-day business life. The book was written with people just starting or thinking of starting a business career in mind. But, whatever level you're at today and whatever level you hope to progress to, you may find things in here that you already knew, but just don't follow every day. We all need an occasional reminder of what's right. And lastly, hopefully, you'll find some of the anecdotes interesting if not entertaining.

Why did I write the book? Part of it was vanity and to challenge myself to see if I could do it. But it was more about putting my ideas out there for others to consider. I find most books on management and business leadership too onerous to understand and slog through, usually introducing some new complex model you have to learn and then apply. I think life and business, as a part of life, are much simpler. They both take hard work and focus, but you don't need a bunch of charts and jargon to get by.

I thought a simple book, written in the style of casual conversations and advice from an uncle figure, might best convey some of what I've learned in 40 years. Is what I've written the Gospel? No, just my view based on the experiences I've had over the years.

The book is in the form of conversations on a variety of related topics. As you read it, envision yourself sitting around the table after a big family dinner, or on the front porch on a summer evening, listening to some stories and advice from your favorite uncle. Occasionally I'll insert a question in *italics* from an imaginary reader to keep us all in the moment of a quiet conversation.

One caveat, this book is intended for those who want to advance and get something done. If you just want to collect a check, hide amongst the masses and bitch about the boss or the company, my advice won't be of much use to you. If you want to accomplish things, lead rather than follow, and make an impact, then please stay tuned.

I'm writing this book not with a narrow focus, but a very broad perspective. While the stories told are based on my experiences, I believe you'll find the core points of the conversations relevant, even if the illustrative cases (stories) used to illustrate them aren't consistent with your experiences. One last note, due to restrictions from some nondisclosure agreements and sometimes so as not to embarrass anybody, I occasionally use pseudonyms for the names of companies and people.

Background

After graduating with an MBA from the University of Florida in 1982, I began my career with Arthur Andersen & Co. (AA) in their Management Information Consulting Division (MICD), now called Accenture. At the time, AA was one of the premier accounting firms and their MICD was a leader in the small but fast-growing information technology space. For simplicity, let's call this employer what we did back then, the Firm.

The Firm was known for hiring folks right out of college and then training them in their methods and ways. We had no bad habits to break, only the Firm's way to learn.

During my time with the Firm, I had the opportunity to work on a host of projects, large and small, across a number industries and in a number of locales.

We were trained in the Firm's ways, not just in terms of processes, but also in terms of culture. Competitors would negatively say we were clones, but that was nonsense. There was plenty of debate within the organization on projects, plans, strategies, and personnel. But, that debate stayed inside. Once we faced the outside world, it was as a united force.

In addition, since we were all trained in the same way, inoculated with the same culture even, it was simple to put together teams of people from offices all over the country and even the world. We spoke the same language and in minutes could be communicating and working together as if we had known each other for years instead of having just met.

    I remember later in my career, long after leaving the Firm, I was with another consulting company, Adjoined, that employed a fair number of Firm alumni. I was part of a team sent out to pitch new business to Estée Lauder at their Long Island office in New York state. We were late to the process, as I had just joined the company and unearthed the opportunity from one of my old contacts. To be generous, we were flying a little blind.

    In any case, I and four other people from three other offices showed up at the meeting. None of us had ever met before and I think only two of us had even spoken to each other on the phone previously. We took a quick minute while getting coffee and talked about the order of the discussion and who would focus on what. Then we went in to present to the Estée Lauder team.

    As I said, we were late to the process and the Estée Lauder team was only taking the meeting as a favor to their new chief information officer (CIO), who was a former coworker of mine. I started with a general overview of our organization and then moved into discussion of the issue at hand, implementing the enterprise software application SAP.

    At that point, you would have thought our team had been practicing and working together for years. We finished each other's sentences, seamlessly moved through all the critical areas, with each of us contributing their expertise.

At the end, the Estée Lauder team was quite impressed. But, they felt we were still too small to take on such a big project for them. They chose a global consultancy, then hired us to watch over that company. Within two months the other company was gone and it was our project. Nice win for Adjoined and a nice win for me to be able to have the contacts to get us in the door. It was a good way to start a new job.

I bring this story up here because many of the things I discuss in this book are lessons I initially learned while working at the Firm.

While the Firm had its way of doing things, it was also a business with a need to serve clients. Those of us on the front lines had to have some innate skills of our own in order to survive. We had to be quick on our feet, flexible, and open to taking prudent risks. And, since we were always being thrown into new situations, we had to have ways to learn fast while appearing expert the whole time. My chosen method was listening, which you'll read more about in Conversation 4.

After leaving the Firm, I joined Ryder System, a Fortune 500 company, in their information technology (IT) department as a group manager. In my five years there, I quickly rose to the director and then vice president levels and being responsible for all IT services for Ryder Transportation Services (RTS, a $3 billion division) and the parent company.

There I got to see the corporate world from the inside, something I had not been able to do as a consultant, and got firsthand exposure to the unique pressures that public companies are under and the issues involved with turning a large ship.

The first project I took on at Ryder was leading a team to create a shared services center (SSC) for the company. The objective was to consolidate 100 small district administrative offices into a single service center. The trick was to do this without investing in new systems. To accomplish this, we had to pick a site, so we chose Alpharetta, Georgia, just north of Atlanta, as the place to build an office. We then had to design revised processes, craft a solution to dump the 100 small AS/400s and consolidate onto a small set of larger processors (thanks to IBM for their help), and deal with any number of other technical, process, policy, construction and personnel matters.

I still remember the day when "Bob," whose sole function seemed to be to fly to headquarters each week and wander the halls, sidled up to me and said, "Gary, I see issues."

My reaction was this: "Bob, I'm up to my ass in issues; I need solutions." And, solutions is what we found – no thanks, by the way, to Bob. You're likely to run into your own "Bob" during your career.

In the end, we opened the shared services center in less than nine months and it is still in operation to this day, 25 years later.

After leaving Ryder in 2000, I started my own consultancy, Urban Partners, Inc. (UPi), which has remained in business these past 20 years. UPi's mission is to provide senior-level / global consultancy-level experience to small and midsize companies tailored in a way that fits their situation and price point.

While operating UPi, I have on occasion taken advantage of opportunities for me to personally join other companies while UPi continued to operate for the primary benefit of my associate members. I did this twice, both times to learn new skills and participate in equity opportunities. This has included my time with a company called Adjoined, where we were able to sell the business twice within a four-year period, and more recently, a life sciences company, specifically a contract research organization (CRO), Clinical, where I held a C-level position and was the strategic architect behind an operating environment that differentiated the company and provided the spark for an increased valuation during an acquisition by private equity investors.

Throughout this period, I continued to learn what did and did not work, adding numerous new companies, industries and locations to my experience. As of this writing, I estimate conservatively to have worked hands-on with more than 50 different companies or government agencies, in more than 25 states and 10 different countries.

I can't say I've had nothing but success throughout my career. I've had my share of wins and a few losses along the way. In fact, I'd say if someone claims never to have lost, then they must not have played, or might have just played in the minor leagues with unskilled opposition.

As I mentioned earlier, I was with the Firm for 13 years. Why so long? Because the prize of partnership was always tantalizingly close. In fact, I was designated a partner for about five days early in the beginning of my thirteenth year. I was told I was in, introduced to a client as the new partner taking over the account, and even went to that client's board meeting representing the Firm. A few days later, it was, "We changed our minds, we needed to cut the [partner] list. Would you like to try again?" My response was uh, no thanks, I'll go find something else.

In spite of that bait-and-switch treatment, I didn't bear a grudge, I wasn't happy, but life sometimes serves you lemons.

In this book, my goal is to distill what I've learned these past 40 years so that you can have a head start in your own journey. I try to illustrate each of my points with stories from my own career. Some stories may have applied to more than one of the conversations, but I tried to use them where I felt they were the best match.

At some points, you may find yourself saying, "I already know that." Maybe you do know it, but do you live it every day? And maybe you know it, but didn't know if others felt the same way. A little validation can be a good thing.

I believe the points in this book are relevant to anyone regardless of gender identity, race, religion, ethnic background, or sexual orientation. I am aware others will face additional and/or different hurdles than I did.

Lastly, any experience I relate, positive or negative, is only as it relates to the specific story I am relaying. It in no way reflects on the overall qualifications or practices of the individuals or companies involved. They are only what I saw at that time and place and are used here only to illustrate the larger points covered in each Conversation.

Thank you for taking the time to read my musings. I hope you enjoy them and have an "aha" moment or two. Keep in mind as you read my thoughts that this isn't meant to be a Harvard Business School textbook. Instead, think of it as some savvy advice from an aging, but far from dead, uncle.

Life is terribly short; you don't realize it till it's too late. If you spend all your time looking for wrongs and slights, you'll find them. People are far from perfect. But while you're doing that, time marches on and life goes on without you. Take time to live.

Conversation 1 – Embrace Goals

To begin with, in this Conversation I'm talking about business goals, not personal goals. I'm not here to speak to the benefits of goal setting in one's personal life. That is a subject for another book. What's written here pertains to goals in business.

First, I'll state unequivocally, ALL businesses need to have goals. They may be just financial goals, they may be some combination of financial and other things, but they need to exist. If the company you work for doesn't have any goals, you need to go find another job. Or, if you're the one responsible for setting goals, well, set them!

If the company does have goals and you're not the CEO, then you need to know those goals and make sure that your department, area, or span of control has goals that are aligned with and in support of the overall company goals.

As the old adage says, "If you don't know where you're going, any road will get you there." To which I would add, "and in business, when you get there you won't like it." Without goals, setting the markers against which you can measure progress, ensuring alignment across the business, and providing some lamppost to guide you, you're just wandering in the darkness. Any success that does find you will be fleeting, not repeatable, and ultimately not satisfying, as you won't be able to point to what you did to deserve it.

But don't despair; without goals, you're unlikely to have to deal with the effects of undeserved success, imposter syndrome and such. You're more likely to be dealing with bankruptcy lawyers, unemployment applications, and depression.

As a side note, I must admit that I have participated in a business where even without goals we were able to generate a little success and accomplish the partial sale of the business. However, the chickens did come quickly home to roost as we were unable to repeat, let alone build on, the previous success, resulting in a massive restructure/layoff. To quote Lincoln, "You can fool some of the people some of the time, but you can't fool all of the people all of the time."

Now, you could probably fill a small library with all the books on goal setting, goal seeking, strategic planning, goals vs. objectives, and on and on it goes. If your company doesn't have a process to set goals, find a book that fits you and use it. Just do it now.

Whichever process you follow, there are just a few important points you should remember.

Goals should be aspirational – bold – motivating. A goal to grow revenues by 1%, which is likely lower than inflation, may be achievable, but it won't excite anyone, or result in creative solutions or prudent risk taking. And, if adopted for more than a short transitional period, it will likely lead to the end of the business.

No, you want goals that cause everyone to sit up and take notice. To think, *how will we ever get there?* – hell, to cause *you* to ask that question. Those types of goals will drive you and your teams to start really thinking, applying yourselves, and moving the business forward.

Once you've set your goals, leave them alone. Goals should be stable. You're going to use your goals as markers on the horizon, searchlights guiding you through the darkness. That won't work if they're forever moving. It would be a much different world if navigators couldn't have relied on the North Star in the days before GPS.

In business, goals need to be developed in such a way that they can remain stable and relevant. Don't make them overly trendy or so short-term that you can't make any meaningful progress toward achieving them before they change. You'll need to derive and adopt detailed business plans after setting your goals. That activity will take time. Then, it will take even more time to execute those plans and measure progress. In my experience, 3-5 year goals are best.

To summarize, this means don't develop goals based on the trends of the moment, don't make them excessively detailed, and don't make them easy to change. Do make them sustainable, worthwhile, and important to the company's success.

Hey, but what happens if things change in the environment and your goals become outdated or unachievable no matter what you do?

Now, that's a very good question.

Doing normal times, your goals should stretch your capabilities and force you to develop ways to shore up any weaknesses and exploit your strengths. But, as we saw with COVID-19, some unforeseen event from the outside can upset the whole applecart.

First off, if you have a good, solid set of goals and have metrics that you're tracking, then at least you'll immediately start seeing how the change is affecting you. That might not sound like much, but if you're in a dark room filled with sharp knives and deep pits, a little light – no matter how feeble – can be very useful.

Second, if you've been a diligent planner, then you have the skills to reassess the realities on the ground and start developing new plans. Note I said *plans*, not goals. You want to keep your goals steady. You might have to tack away from them in the moment, but you still want them marking success whenever it's feasible to turn back. Plans, on the other hand, are the means used to achieve your goals. Goals define where you want to end up at some point in the future, plans are how you will get there.

This revised planning exercise will involve a certain amount of triage, casting certain things overboard as you try to keep the ship afloat. Here again, having a steady set of goals can help you determine what will get you the most bang for the buck. What can you lose that will help but still not damage the strategic vision and achievement of the goals?

Lastly, while the exact nature of an abnormal event may be a surprise, the fact that something out of the ordinary happened should not be a surprise. If you're in business, you have to keep aware of what's going on in the broader world.

You need to develop at least a shell of a plan for what you'll do if disaster strikes: a business continuity plan. That plan, even if it's just a page of bullet-pointed actions to take, can be a lifesaver. It will help stop any immediate bleeding, and give you courage and a feeling of being in control, which can be all the difference you need to survive while others fall.

Illustrative Cases:

I'll give you three brief stories. One of the places I worked had an annual process to develop a strategic plan. Now re-read that sentence because words matter. Their annual strategic planning process was set up to develop – not revise/extend/modify – a strategic plan that would be in place for several years. How can you operate a business where the overall strategic plan (where goals are written down) is rewritten every year? You can't. What happened in this case is everyone went through the planning process and then went back to whatever they were doing because the plan was just a document to file away and a box for someone to check off on their Management by Objective (MBO) annual personnel review.

At another company, the chairman had a goals document which he did share with members of the management team. But, after that, there was no follow-through. Nobody was expected to develop plans aligned with the goals. No objective measures were developed and tracked to gauge progress. The goals never came up in any discussion as to how whatever project or process being debated would help us achieve our goals.

So, while we had goals, nobody bothered to turn on the lighthouse and we all sailed our different ways until the ship of state eventually smashed into the reef and started taking on water. Even then, the goals were not looked to for guidance. The emergency horn was sounded and everyone either stampeded for a lifeboat or drowned below decks.

    A story demonstrating being overly trendy, at the company with the annual strategic plan, the determination was made in the late 1990s that we needed to be on the internet conducting e-commerce, because that was the buzzword of the day. Now today, this would be without a question a true statement. But in the late '90s we just didn't have the broadband technology, smartphones, or application development tools to really support online commerce. But, that wasn't going to stop us! We were going to the World Wide Web! I still remember getting a call from our president, wanting me to return early from a business trip in San Francisco to meet with a prospective investment opportunity. I ended up ditching my meetings with critical suppliers to fly the red-eye back to Miami to make the meeting. Sleep deprived and juiced up on coffee, I remember being shocked when a young guy walked into the conference room in tennis shoes and jeans. (Today I'd be shocked if a tech executive wasn't dressed like that.

    This guy was the founder of the company that wanted our investment. He pitched an application that independent truck drivers could connect to when they were at truck stops. The application would allow them to play some games, send email messages, and check online maps. Later it would expand as other items became available online.

Never mind that we did not do business with independent truck drivers, didn't own truck stops and really didn't have any direct way to monetize this or build it in to our existing services. The only question was: Is it technically feasible? When I was asked for my view on the viability of the technical solution, all I could say was yes, it could obviously work, but I also asked what was in it for us. Everyone went with the first part of my statement and ignored the question. The guy got his money, we got nothing, and I guess everyone was happy, because we were invested in the World Wide Web.

Well gee, Gary, you just shared two stories of not having goals or not using goals for their intended purpose. How about one where goals did prove their value?

Good point. And here is the story.

At one point I left my own consulting business and joined a larger, but still small consultancy, Adjoined Consulting. Adjoined had been started by some former coworkers from my days with the Firm and was trying to create a smaller version of the Firm. I joined them because their size and resources would allow me to stay more current in technology and business, and it afforded me some equity that, according to plan, would at some point be convertible to cash.

Both of my objectives were achieved. I gained valuable experience and we were able to sell the business. Technically we sold it twice, once to another slightly larger consultancy and then both those components to a global consultancy, Capgemini. This not only allowed me to get some cash but to get a little premium and get it fully paid out much faster than the first deal provided for.

After the second sale, I did decide that Capgemini and a large consultancy wasn't the learning and growing environment I wanted. I was running a string of consultants. I didn't get to work with clients, and even the people I managed weren't really mine to grow and mentor. They were just products to move off the shelves.

Now to the tie-in to our topic, Goals. After leaving Capgemini, I restarted my consulting practice. About a year later the principals who had started Adjoined (Rodney and Kevin) also left Capgemini and started a new venture. Virtustream was established as an Infrastructure as a Service (IaaS) business with a focus on enterprise systems, primarily SAP. Essentially, they were setting out to build a cloud solution for folks to run their big corporate systems on.

I joined as a consultant to initially help with setting up some basic operations infrastructure, accounting and customer relationship management (CRM) solutions. I then morphed into a role of leading the North American operations and sales teams.

From the beginning, Virtustream had set very specific goals and then put in place specific methods and processes to track and report on progress toward achieving these goals. And, that's what we did. Weekly, detailed tracking on the various metrics that supported the achievement of the overall company goals.

We reviewed reports line by line. Any missed targets were discussed and action plans developed to get back on track ASAP. From the top there was consistent and continuous emphasis on the targets, achieving the goals, and taking action to address any shortfall and get back on track. No one was ever allowed to take their eye off the ball. A missed target, no matter how minor, was reason for a serious dressing down by the chairman. And, in case anyone tried to sandbag and just set lower targets, the strategic plan was there, ever watchful, with its list of very specific targets and goals. If you weren't going to get the $100K sale from Company A, where were you going to get it? If not today, it better be tomorrow, and even then you were late and subject to some serious commentary on your intelligence, heritage and worthiness as a person. Not fun, but bit by bit the machine ground on, meeting more and more goals, pushing aside all excuses and obstacles.

Unfortunately, I found that the role I'd been given wasn't right for me. Given where it was in its early development stage, the company needed someone with way more detailed technical SAP and infrastructure skills than I had. I recognized this and we parted friends.

The company, following the guiding light of their goals, went on to be acquired for more than $1 billion. A testament to the skills of the team and the vision of the founders to set goals and then meticulously keep everyone focused and moving toward those goals even when the goals were way out ahead of current realities.

To be fair, I didn't agree 100% with some of the motivational tools used to get people to perform. A little too much yelling and name-calling for my taste. As I talk about in Conversation 7 – It Isn't Personal, you will need to have a thick skin at times. But still, as the general method of management, success notwithstanding, I don't think yelling and intimidation tactics should ever be the go-to play.

In conclusion:
    a. Goals are the points in the future that you want to get to – generally 3-5 years out.
    b. Goals should be awe inspiring but still achievable with effort.
    c. Plans with targets and metrics are the tactical tools used to manage day-to-day.
    d. You have to manage closely, every day, and hold yourself accountable.
    e. Wandering aimlessly doesn't lead anywhere and is not a repeatable process to achieve success.

Conversation 2 – Decide and Move

Now that you have goals sitting out there to guide you to success, you have to do something. Sitting around in meetings re-reading the strategic plan isn't going to help you achieve it. Action must be taken, customers need to be served, marketing needs to market, sales needs to sell, and support functions need to do their part to not only deliver services but continually improve on the quality and cost of those services. All of these things require motion. No one ever won a race by not moving, even the tortoise.

When I refer to "Move," I'm trying to say decide and take action. I don't mean get up from your desk every 20 minutes and exercise for your health. That's a good thing, but not what I'm referring to here. Moving is making a decision and doing something.

But I just joined the company, what can I possible do? Nobody's going to let me decide anything. Well, that depends. Doing something doesn't have to be big and bold, it can be small, incremental even, but it needs to be something. As you grow in your career, you might hear someone described as having a bias for action. Be one of those people. They get stuff done and are moving. Moving the business forward and moving their careers up.

If you just started, ask to see your team's plan for the year. Understand it and then, as you're given new tasks, make sure they are somehow linked to achieving the plan. If you don't understand, seek guidance.

One more point: As with the Conversation about goals, this Conversation is intended to share my experience in business. Doing something, in my view, is always better than doing nothing. I recognize that might not be the right approach in other areas of life. Medicine comes to mind, where the maxim is "first do no harm." Or government, which probably should adopt the same maxim as medicine.

If you have great ideas, creative plans, or a crisis to address, not making a decision and starting to move is absolutely the worst thing you can do. You have to believe in yourself (see Conversation 8). If you don't, well, as the saying goes, "stay on the porch and let the big dogs hunt."

If I ever do a road show, my vision has always been to have each seat fitted with a cushion and a note reading "For Inspirational Message Turn Over." Once turned over, the other side would read: "Get Off Your ASS and Do Something!"

Too many people spend way too much time waiting for orders, getting trapped in what's called decision paralysis, or avoiding being tasked with anything in the first place. "But I have to do some analysis first." True. Just don't take too long. Prudent analysis and review is appropriate, but that can't become your life's work. Whatever business you're in, management wants decisions made and actions taken that contribute to the company's success. You'll have to become comfortable making those decisions in less time and with fewer facts than you would like.

Remember, this book is advice for folks wanting to get ahead and advance. If you're one of those people, you can't hide from making decisions. Orders from above often don't arrive and who's to say the person giving direction has a clue what he or she is doing. Meaning, there may not always be someone to tell you what to do or tell you what to do in a timely manner. You'll need to think and act on your own.

Don't be one of the "waiters." If you have career aspirations, move. Trust me, if you're in the boat and not rowing, you'll find yourself on shore, or worse, in the water, soon enough.

Bottom line, it all starts with starting. You have to make a decision and begin to move. Ideally forward toward your goals, but be prepared to turn and even backtrack as necessary. Just keep moving, don't ever stop and become frozen with indecision.

To illustrate the point, as a consultant one of your routine functions is responding to requests for proposals (RFPs). Sometimes you win, but sometimes you don't. When you don't win, many salespeople's reaction is to vent for a while back at the office, blame some lower-level staffer for their graphics, and blame finance for setting too high a margin requirement. While those are actions, they're not really doing something in the sense of moving your company toward winning more deals.

Doing something would entail calling the client and asking why? What did we miss? Was it our price? And so on. It could also involve getting your hands on the winning proposal and seeing what it had that yours did not. Now, you might be saying, *how would I ever get that?* Well, first thing to do is ask the client (we'll cover this more in Conversation 7). If you've got any kind of a relationship, you'll be shocked to see how open they'll be. If when you call them they tell you to pound sand or won't take your call, then you should know that the issue is you didn't work the sales process correctly (a subject for another book).

In any case, whatever results from reaching out will put you in a better position for the next RFP and provide you insights to help convince finance the margins are too high.

A secondary benefit from moving is people are energized by movement. Have you ever gone down to the beach before a storm and watched the waves roll in? Or watched a horse race? Movement creates excitement which affects everyone. How many times have you cringed on a "slow" day when you realized it was only 10:00 and you were already itching to get out to lunch?

Having projects, things to do – particularly when they are aligned with the goals of the company – is the best HR incentive you can have.

Illustrative Cases:

Here's a story from the consulting world. One of the metrics you track in that space is employee turnover. A certain amount -- you pick the amount -- is healthy, because you want fresh blood and you want to have underperformers' self-select out. But you don't want so much turnover that it impacts your ability to staff projects, provide training, and sell new work because of a loss of experience.

What's interesting and relevant to our discussion on movement is that when you review the data, there is always an uptick in attrition when business is a little slow. People with time on their hands become bored and anxious. This feeling then puts them into the job market where some competitor can snatch them up. To avoid that, always have projects, even internal projects or putting folks on client projects at no or reduced costs to keep them busy and engaged. Just make sure those projects are still aligned with the overall goals for the company.

Here's a travel-related story to illustrate my point about the need to move. I would conservatively guess I've flown some 3 million or more miles. Hundreds and hundreds of flights at all times of the year. And, I'm very proud to say you would have never seen me on the nightly news as one of those sad-looking creatures stuck sleeping at the airport when the big blizzard shuts things down. Why? Not because I haven't had flights canceled, rerouted, or aborted in flight. No, I just don't allow myself to get stuck.

One time I was returning to Miami from Estée Lauder's Long Island office. It was winter and snow was predicted. I got to New York's LaGuardia airport and it was already snowing pretty heavily. As soon as I entered the airport, I saw my flight was "Delayed." Now, I could have checked my bag, gone out to the gate or maybe the airline club and waited until the airline told me something. But, I knew airlines never tell you anything in a timely manner, and if the flight was delayed now with the snow on the ground and still falling, it wasn't going to be un-delayed with more snow.

Instead, I turned around, walked back out, grabbed a passing cab, and went into the city. I got myself a room at the New York Hilton, where I heard reports that the airports were all shut down and I could see that even cabs were becoming scarce. I went up to my room, freshened up and then walked the two blocks to a great steak restaurant on a side street just down from the Ed Sullivan Theater.

I spent a lovely night in Manhattan, and flew out the next morning, enjoying the bright blue skies and snow-covered ground. Had I not decided and moved when I did, I likely would not have gotten a cab and then ended up stranded at the airport, waking up next to a wastebasket with my suit rumpled and my neck twisted and stiff.

A last story to demonstrate movement is my experience at Clinical and the development of TALOS, our proprietary operating environment. Even though it was the stated objective of the chairman to have TALOS and it was peppered throughout our marketing, there were still several leaders in the company who weren't in favor. It's not that they had an alternative solution, it was they were just negative. You run into these folks sometimes.

Wait, what the hells a TALOS??

That's a brilliant question, the answer is a little complicated. So, let me digress for just a moment and describe the TALOS vision to you. TALOS was to be a process-driven, automated solution that would guide and manage a clinical trial from start to finish. This would ensure maximum efficiency, accuracy, and auditability. Through the use of TALOS, employees would be guided every step of the way on a trial. They would have their own personal task list presented to them each day along with whatever documentation they needed to complete or information they needed to gather in order to complete a task. Late tasks would be quickly identified and escalated until they were resolved. Missing documentation would be flagged and metrics would be collected on each individual employee. Further, the tasks and documentation would be tied to the regulatory compliance processes of the company and would adjust if those process were changed.

This automation of basic mechanics is very doable, while a little more sophistication would be required to then adapt to outside forces and/or address one-off situations that could arise in the real world. For this we envisioned a serious of "what if" instruction guides that again could be presented to employees for their use. Later, those could be turned into some sort of artificial intelligence (AI) functionality, but my goal was to start small.

Now I happened to believe in the chairman's vision and was going to do what I could to achieve it, given the constraints of time and money that we had. So, instead of seeking to endlessly debate the negative nellies, I set out to build TALOS. Brick by brick, piece by piece, I and my small team constructed something that, while never fully completed during my tenure, moved us far enough down the road that during the due diligence to sell the business we received high marks from the technical team reviewing it and established TALOS as something that is still the cornerstone of the company's marketing efforts.

A specific instance of what I'm talking about is the trial database. No matter how we addressed the issues of AI or dealt with integrating the processes with the TALOS software, we needed to have all the basic demographic data related to a trial stored somewhere. I thought, why wait? So I had my team build it and we got an immediate benefit. We now had a single place, available to every employee that listed all the trials we were doing along with basic demographics of what it was, who the sponsor was, who the project manager was, etc. This was something we had never had before. While the naysayers wanted to just sit and complain and worry about how we were going to solve issue #14,153, I just decided what was of value regardless, could be done quickly, and would get us one more step toward the ultimate goal.

A final point on TALOS is that along with the negative nellies, I had to contend with the flyover visionaries. These are the folks that fly at great heights and have stupendous visions (perhaps from the lack of oxygen at altitude) and then spew those visions on all those below working in the fields. We brought some of them into the business. You need a sturdy umbrella to contend with the resulting deluge.

The issue with them was not that their visions were unsound, it's just they ignored the realities on the ground. As a business we only had so much money to spend, support from operations was zero, and we were always facing competing pressures of real-world problems to address first.

It would have been nice and easy to develop TALOS if it had been a standalone software business; then we'd have just built the product. That wasn't the case. I know I moved the needle in a positive direction, and now it's up to somebody else to take it from there.

In conclusion:
    a. Doing something is always better than doing nothing.
    b. It starts with you deciding to move, and having a bias for action.
    c. People are energized when they're moving.
    d. Those who sit still will get passed by and eventually run over.

Conversation 3 – Know the Safe Exits

Whenever you undertake an initiative of any size or complexity, there will be a level of uncertainty and risk. If you try to plan in order to eliminate all uncertainty and risk, you'll never do anything, and as we said in Conversation 2, that's not good.

Recognizing then that there are risks and uncertainties, you need to keep your eyes open for the exits. How can you get out of the situation if things don't work? How can you achieve partial success and salvage something? Can you orchestrate a strategic retreat, assuming you didn't burn the village you just left? Or, can you otherwise make the proverbial lemonade out of lemons?

Failure to have some safe exits – call them contingency plans if you want – can leave you between the rock and a hard place. Marching forward might be impossible or extravagantly costly and going back might not be possible. If you get in that position, start a new resume.

But, in the conversation we had on goals, you said we might have a boss who demands we meet the targets regardless -- how does that square with safe exits?

Nice catch, you've been paying attention. Yes, you do need to meet targets and move continually toward goals. What we're talking about here is extricating ourselves from a bad situation as best we can. A maxim you can use in almost any bad situation is this: The first thing to do if you find yourself in a hole is quit digging. Once you do that, crawl out of the hole and find yourself a new way to get rapidly back on the target-meeting, goal-attainment express.

Remember, any undertaking of significance will come with risk. You won't be able to eliminate all the risk, and time and money are always in short supply. To protect yourself and help ensure some value comes from the effort, you need to plan for safe exits, points you could get to and get partial value, ways you can pause and buy more time to get work done, or ways to unwind what was done without having spent all the money. All of this planning is what I call knowing the safe exits.

Illustrative Cases:

As a demonstration of this situation, I can call on the very painful memories of an accounts receivable (AR) system implementation gone awry. As consultants, we were asked by a longtime client to help them with a new AR system they had to put in to complete the separation from their former parent company. We scoped the work at let's say $1 million, but they only had $300K to spend. They suggested that they would handle all the design, project management, and planning work and just wanted us to support some of the technical aspects. Unfortunately, we said yes.

As the project got rolling, there were a couple of key issues. First they would move from the manual application of payments to an automated approach, and second, they would convert both their regions and all accounts simultaneously. Given the complexities of the automated application of payments, we advised a small pilot vs. a big bang. We were overruled.

To further complicate matters, as the project was still in development, the CEO announced the layoffs of the entire AR staff and provided no incentive for them to stay on and assist in the design of the new system. Headquarters (HQ) finance staff then took on the task of designing the processes and algorithms for the payment matching.

When it came time to go live, all hell broke loose. Payments were allocated seemingly randomly. The amount of money in suspense grew exponentially each day, and even many payments allocated to specific accounts turned out to be misapplied. In this case, with no AR staff left, it was impossible to go back to manual payment allocation. I won't bore you with the details, but this disaster went on for weeks until it was finally solved with a mix of additional staff to do manual application with a very limited automated process.

The lack of an exit strategy, failing to do a pilot for a small test of real data, and firing the AR staff in advance of system go-live and not incentivizing them to stay on and help, all created a mess that cost the company money and customer satisfaction.

As the smoke cleared and the damage assessment was done, we learned that some of the root causes were a second AR system maintained in the desk drawers of the AR staff members that were fired. They kept manual records (in their own unique codes) that tracked how certain accounts paid their invoices, which stops belonged to which accounts (the accounts traded stops amongst themselves but those changes were never reflected in the master database), which customer checking accounts were meant for which stops, and so on. Good information to have if you plan to automate.

The CEO who was largely responsible for this cluster did avail himself of the CEO's Privilege, the maxim that a CEO can always blame others for the company's failures. It's sad to see how many play this game and how many times they get away with it. There is no logic to it. If the staff (employee or consultant) was inept or otherwise messed up, who put them in that position in the first place? When you get to the top, promise me that if something ever goes bad on your watch you'll stand up, put on your big-person clothes and take responsibility. I don't suggest going as far as the Japanese, but just admit you had a hand in the mess. Then go back in and fight to fix it, and find that way to create some lemonade.

As for the CEO and his AR complaints, he was wrong and I'll happily debate him if he's still around. Why? A) We weren't hired to manage the effort or design the solution. B) When we offered advice it was willfully ignored. C) They made some of the dumbest errors by firing people in the middle of a project with no plan to retain knowledge. D) It became clear nobody had been managing AR for years, letting the clerks become the only ones with a clue about how things worked. E) They did not know their customer – even who owned which stops.

One last point about having an exit strategy. Don't advertise it. If you let people know they don't have to worry because we can easily undo this or go a different direction, they won't fight to achieve the task at hand. Keep your fallback plans quiet, and shared on a need-to-know basis.

A little story here. At a recent employer, one of the first things I wanted done after I joined was to move the systems off of some on-premises servers and into the cloud. We were operating out of the ninth floor of a glass office building in sight of the Atlantic Ocean in South Florida. Not a great design. Glass windows break and drywall crumbles when hurricanes come through, plus the ninth floor happened to be the top floor. Believe it or not, those office tower roofs leak on a good day and water can really roll in during a storm. A storm of any size could easily cause significant damage to our server room, knocking us offline and leaving us with significant downtime while we sourced new equipment and a place to house it. We had to do something, and my decision was to move to the cloud, specifically Amazon Web Services (AWS).

Once I had made that decision, I had to make another decision.

How much do I tell people?

Exactly, and usually the answer is as little as you can get away with. In this case, from previous experience, I knew that anything that impacts someone's physical proximity to the server can cause them to drive you crazy with phantom "performance" complaints. Years earlier when I was with Ryder, we had a group of data entry personnel who entered transportation trip records. Heads-down data entry. Their manager was so fixated on their productivity that they weren't even allowed to have phones on their desks.

As we worked on the shared services center at Ryder (which I described back in the Introduction), they became one of the groups targeted to be moved to Atlanta. This unleashed endless rounds of meetings and debates, with the issue eventually getting escalated all the way to the CFO's desk.

To avoid a fight, he said leave them be. A few years later when we outsourced IT infrastructure to IBM, we moved the mainframe they were connected to from down the hall in Miami headquarters to Raleigh Durham. North Carolina. Nobody said a word about performance.

Now fast-forward to Clinical and the need to move to the cloud. I didn't want to refight the performance wars or have 200 people blaming every typo in their reports on the cloud. So, I determined to not only keep my exit strategy quiet, I kept the whole move quiet. With the help of my IT director, we did things under the heading of a pilot program. As the project progressed, I never told anyone switching back was as easy as literally plugging a cable back in. Nor did I tell them just who or how much was involved in the pilot. I compared it to a double-blind study which they understood and accepted. I didn't want them to think we could go any direction but forward. If we needed the cable plugged in, I knew where it was and that was enough.

We completed the conversion as planned, nobody was negatively impacted, and very few knew anything really changed. Being in the cloud had several benefits: it made our audits much simpler, made the move to the new office a much easier effort for IT with zero downtime, eliminated some persistent complaining from offshore offices about performance and, as it turns out, when COVID-19 struck, the decision to move to the cloud appeared to be a stroke of genius. Now there are many claiming to having come up with the idea.

Lastly, one more story of having an exit strategy. Again at Clinical, our office lease was expiring at the end of October 2019. Because we had been busy with the sale of the business in 2018, we hadn't taken any action regarding new space. We did know that we needed more of it (at least at that time we did) and we knew that the existing building was sold out.

Starting in January, we began interviewing real estate management companies to help us with the selection of space and the process to get it leased and us in it. As we started each meeting, the first question the prospective provider would ask is "when is your current lease up?" Every time we said "October," they made a face and said "You really should have started at least six months ago." Well, we couldn't unwind the clock, so all we could do was soldier on.

Yours truly was anointed by the chairman to do the soldiering while he tried to deal with the new owners and some blips in the business. Now, if any of you have ever bought a house with another person, imagine doing that with 200 people. Each with their own opinions on where, how much, how tall, what shape, what color, etc., etc. Fortunately the chairman and I had come up with some ground rules. First, we would stay in the immediate vicinity of the existing office. Anyone who took a job with us knew where the office was. It seemed unfair to pick it up and move it on them. It didn't hurt that the chairman and I each lived within view of the office; we were just looking out for everyone else. And, second, we wanted a light, bright, open design. The existing office had belonged to a financial brokerage firm and we had taken it over as-is. It looked like a 1950s version of an office. Dark wood everywhere, offices on exterior walls blocking any light getting to the inner offices.

Given those parameters and the fact we wanted roughly 30,000 square feet, there weren't too many options. All the real estate firms we were talking to about helping us with the deal brought us the same set of building prospects.

Unfortunately for me, there was more than one choice of location. In my view, there was one clear winner, but the necessity to have at least two for negotiating leverage suddenly became an endless negotiation as we went back and forth between two contenders. All the time, the days were falling off the calendar. Each option had various alternatives to try to get us in by the end of October and our existing landlord did agree to go month-to-month if necessary to give us some breathing space. We did use that, staying until mid-December.

But, I was uncomfortable with those scenarios and made my own plans in case of an emergency. If we couldn't get in the new space and the landlord changed his mind, which he could if he got a new tenant wanting to move, we needed an option. I decided our option was go remote and have all the employees work from home. Which, with the COVID-19 pandemic, we ended up doing in 2020.

However, in this case I kept my plans to myself. There was no reason to bring it up and start having the naysayers and bleacher crowd pick at it. It was truly an emergency plan and in an emergency certain niceties go out the window. The important thing was we'd be able to continue operations regardless of the state of the move. As an aside, we had proved we could do this in 2017 during Hurricane Irma. As most of the peninsula of Florida evacuated, we found our teams scattered as far west as Los Angeles and as far north as Chicago. I myself ended up in Orange Beach, Alabama. A lovely spot and a place I highly recommend, friendliest people you could ever want to meet.

Back on point. However in 2017, we did not have the advantage of the cloud. We still had our old in-house server setup which had to be turned off during the storm. We functioned by having people take what they needed on their laptops, putting three hard disk data backups in the hands of IT and myself so we could email out any documents that someone forgot, and using Outlook email which was on the Microsoft cloud. Not totally efficient, but we stayed open. Now with the AWS cloud, there would be no difference to employees from working in the office.

Ultimately we picked a building, were able to move 60% of the staff in July 2020 and then moved the remainder in December of that year. The space was gorgeous. Perfect for a modern, forward-thinking business. I'm very proud of it. Events got in the way of using it, but hopefully soon folks will be going back to offices and taking advantage of some of the features we built in.

As a final point, if you ever find yourself in charge of the new office design, build or move, make sure you have the architect design you a nice corner office.

In conclusion:
- a. Risk is always with us.
- b. Some plans don't work out, so always have a way out that salvages some good.
- c. Keep exit strategies to yourself as much as possible to keep teams motivated about the main goal.
- d. Exit strategies can include ways to pause parts of the work or deadlines, giving yourself time to complete needed tasks, or standalone blocks of work that can provide value even if the entire project isn't completed.

Conversation 4 - Listening

Listening is the most underrated skill. Think about it. When you see a job posting, what are they always searching for? Presentation skills, verbal communication skills, public speaking, etc. Nobody ever asks whether you are a good listener. I personally find that not only odd, but very damaging to business. If everyone in the room is talking, what's accomplished? Numerous studies have shown that in groups, the talkative ones win the day even when they're wrong. For those of you who've read Stephen Covey's *The 7 Habits of Highly Effective People*, remember that one of the habits is "Seek first to understand, then to be understood." Listen.

All the habits Dr. Covey writes about are critical, but I think listening might be the most important skill you can have in business. Being a good listener requires you to be patient, attentive, empathetic, engaged in the moment, and open minded. To really listen, practically all your senses need to be engaged. Eye and body movements can be just as important as the actual words spoken.

A good listener will be valued. They might not be center stage, but they will be the one those actors turn to for counsel.

You'll often see dominant speakers as leaders; less often it will be someone who is less dynamic. Those are the ones who are the listeners, sucking in information, analyzing it and then acting. Dominant personality types are not necessarily always the right ones to follow.

If you're a talker, you think you have something to say and you want others to listen. But, if you are known as a continuous talker, your audience stops really listening, picks out some part of a point you made, and then spends the rest of their time formulating a response which they fire back at you at the first moment you take a breath. This action then restarts the whole process. Both parties talk past each other with no true exchange of information.

On the other hand, along with listening in order to learn, the advantage of doing more listening than talking is that when you *do* speak, your words carry more weight. If you always have a squeaky noise in the back of your car, over time you'll largely tune it out. But, if your car is always dead quiet while driving and then you get a squeak, you'll notice it and take it to the shop ASAP.

The same logic holds true for people talking. If someone is always talking, you start to tune them out. Even if they say something worthwhile or important, you won't hear it. On the other hand, if someone is usually quiet, reserved even, and then suddenly pipes up with a comment, you hear it and it bears more weight.

Illustrative Cases:

In my own career, I had a chance early on to learn some lessons about this issue, both positive and negative. After four years with Arthur Andersen, you were eligible for early promotion. Long story short – I got passed over. Meanwhile, a peer I was working with on the same project got the early promotion. The difference? He was a nonstop talker, and mostly it was BS. Time after time I'd leave a meeting with him and by the time I got down the hall, I'd be kicking myself for not calling him out on the absolute nonsense he had just spouted nonstop for 20 minutes. But, I was a listener first. I was trying to take in and hear what he was saying and needed about 20 seconds of silence to process it and realize he once again had said nothing. Of course, by then it would be too late, so he looked like a rising star and I looked like another one of the workers, solid, steady but not ready for prime time.

Using what I already knew about moving (see Conversation 2), I did something. I took the Dale Carnegie course. It was a way for me to get out in front of people, learn that everyone has their own story to tell and that everyone is hurting some. Good class, almost like weekly therapy. And, with my outgoing hale and hearty personality, folks who know me now are shocked to think I would have ever needed something like that

Now to close the loop on my peer. A few years after the promotion, he got caught falsifying time and expense documents, a sin he couldn't talk his way out of. I, being the good soldier, was then sent in to finish what he had been working on.

To illustrate the differences between the listener and the talker, let me talk about the two chairmen. Tony Burns, the chairman at Ryder when I was there, was a listener. In meetings he rarely spoke, concentrating on what others were saying and occasionally asking pointed questions seeking clarification.

Tony also had a habit of inviting lower-level executives into his office for one-on-one talks. Having participated in those, I can say the objective was not for Tony to tell you something, it was for you to tell him.

You'd be ushered into Tony's office, where you'd join him at this small conference table. There he'd be, seemingly constantly with a Mountain Dew in his hand, waiting for you. He'd start off with some open-ended question, generally on the area that you'd been told he wanted to talk about. Then after a little conversation, mostly yours, he'd come out of left field with a totally unrelated question.

I remember my first time, we were discussing, or I was updating him on, our Y2K preparedness when he suddenly asked me, "Do you think that shared services center was a good idea?" Since I'd effectively led the team that built it, it was operating fine after more than two years, and I did think it was a good idea, my answer was a resounding "yes" followed by about five minutes of reasons why.

I don't know if he was getting stories from others who were saying it was bad, if he was just fishing, or what, but for what it was worth, he knew my position and why by the time I was done. Now, some folks thought this was some Machiavellian strategy on Tony's part. I found it genius.

With him sitting where he was, who would ever come in and present bad news or less-than-rosy forecasts? The only way he could gather the intelligence that he needed to operate was to listen closely to what people said, how they said it, what they avoided saying, and then asking specific questions to tease out any hidden information and possibly test out his hypothesis. In this way he could make decisions more fully informed and with all the necessary color around an issue. Tony retired in the early 2000s and left behind a company that has over $8 billion in annual revenues today.

The other chairman is Boris, a great guy, and possibly one of the smartest people I have ever met. His life story is truly remarkable and a testament to his skills. He was a Soviet immigrant who came to the US with nothing, and started and sold two multi-million-dollar businesses, creating wealth and opportunity for others along the way. But even he will admit he's not a great listener. He likes to talk.

His thoughts are usually correct and worth hearing. Young and old members of the team can learn from a lot of what Boris has to say and how he says it. But, there came a time when a little more listening would have served Boris better.

His style tended to silence people or confuse them, so that conversations could veer off track with key issues left unresolved. It would also lead to some blind spots that prevented Boris from seeing things as they truly were and not as he wished them to be. Sometimes I wondered if the nonstop talking was purposeful to avoid discussing things he didn't want to or hearing things that contradicted what he wanted. Like all entrepreneurs, his ego was not small and he had a belief that if he wished it so it could be made to happen, whatever it was. A lot of listening and conversation wasn't necessary.

In the end, Boris made three great moves. One, he didn't listen to the head of operations and hired me anyway. Two, he recognized he should listen to me more, and three, when it came time to sell the business, he followed through and listened to me.

But, in day-to-day operations and weekly management meetings, it was all the Boris show. A group of anywhere from five to ten people, depending on who we were calling management that quarter, would meet, get to the first slide or the presentation of the day, and then we were running down some rabbit hole that would consume the rest of the hour. Most of the time, we could have done with less talking, but there were more than a few occasions when Boris was making a very valid assessment and set of suggestions, particularly as it related to the sales process.

In those meetings, the head of sales would have done better to listen (hell, we all would have done better if he had listened). But, he seemed consumed with formulating his response instead of taking in what was being said. He couldn't help it; he was young and an academic. He didn't think like Boris and could not grasp the nuance of things like follow-up. Tossing another email over the transom does not constitute follow-up when one is in sales. He would have been well served had this book existed then.

But the head of sales was also a victim of the unintended side effect mentioned earlier of too much Boris talking. People stop listening -- an issue Boris faced in those management meetings.

As I mentioned earlier, I'm not naturally an outgoing person. But that should not lead you to believe I don't have an ego. No, my friends, I have a huge ego. And I like to be listened to – thus this book. I've just found that in the 40 years I've been working, speaking less but speaking well (being meaningful and on point) gets you further and provides a much bigger positive jolt to the ego.

What do I mean by speaking well? First, speaking facts to the greatest extent possible. To demonstrate the point, a few years ago we were moving to new offices. You'd think everyone would be excited as we'd be going from 19,000 square feet of space where we had four or more people crammed into some offices, to over 30,000 square feet of beautiful, modern space. Unfortunately, the move had to occur in two stages since we could only get half the space to begin with and the remainder to follow about four months later.

As the teams prepared to move, I started to get a lot of pushback about how they would file and research documents in our central file room, which wasn't moving until the second stage. Now, none of these complainers had a solution, but that didn't matter. Again, based on my prior experiences, I knew this would be an issue and had already asked my IT team to give me the data for the past quarter on how many people, and who, used the card reader to enter central files over that time period. The answer was, other than quality assurance (QA), which was staying put for now, nobody. *Really?* Okay, maybe one person every two weeks. With that fact, I didn't have to say a lot.

Now, if the situation doesn't lend itself to specific data like file access, you need to speak logically and rationally. Ranting and emotion won't get people to listen. You can have passion, but don't let it degrade to emotion. A good case to review is a decision that needed the chairman's approval while I was at Ryder. We had Y2K issues to deal with, and one of those was with the old in-house payroll system that was hard to maintain and produced hundreds of errors each pay cycle. We could remediate that system, at some unknown cost over some yet-to-be-determined time frame, or we could put in SAP's payroll system, which our consultants (KPMG – also the corporate auditors) would do for a specific price and would guarantee completion on schedule. We chose the second option, as logical people would.

Neither option was without risk, but when faced with those two choices, why would you ever chose to remediate a system that doesn't work? By the way, our exit strategy was to throw it to ADP if things went to hell on the SAP project. But, my expert friends at KPMG came through and as far as I know, the system is still providing payroll some 21 years later.

Later in my career I did a series of what we called Executive IT Strategic Reviews. Often these were done as part of a private equity company's due diligence or as part of a corporate review of independent divisions. I liked doing them and I was good at it. At one point a peer of mine was tasked with helping me, since the volume of sites was more than I could get to in the desired time frame. After his first one, the client decided they could wait a few extra days to have me do them all myself. *Why?* Here's why.

Coming in as the representative of a potential buyer or corporate parent company can be stressful for the folks you're visiting. I had to make them feel comfortable so that they would open up (even spill their guts, good, bad and ugly) and tell me everything there was to know about their IT.

I had a checklist to help drive the conversation, but I preferred to just tee up areas with broad questions and then let them start talking. I was there to listen, demonstrating empathy (I was a former divisional CIO myself), interest, and knowledge, all in a nonthreatening manner.

Remember, you can also "listen" with more than you ears. Your other senses, particularly your eyes, can collect a wealth of information that can validate what you heard and/or provide new understanding.

My IT review meetings usually took a day, sometimes two due to scheduling. I always managed to include tours of the operations to better understand the business, see the technology in use, and identify where there might be some strategic opportunities.

I saw some fascinating things, an iron pipe foundry where molten iron was poured into molds, spun quickly with a hot cherry-red pipe popping out as the mold opened. I observed the manufacture of fire hydrants and various water valves and the machining and work required to convert blocks of metal into precision parts. I learned where orange juice comes from, even in the off season. (It's frozen in large blocks and stacked up in a cold storage warehouse to be thawed and processed later.) The manufacture of commercial baked goods, that's a little gross.

My listening skills allowed me to see a lot, a lot more than somebody who just wanted to dominate the conversation.

Sometimes what you hear doesn't correspond to what you see. During one of my Executive IT Reviews, in the interview I had been told that the accounts payable (A/P) process had been fully automated and that they did a three-way match of Purchase Order/Receipt/Invoice. As we began our tour and we walked by A/P, all I saw were stacks of paper and people busily going from stack to stack, pulling out documents and stapling them together. This was the three-way match. Apparently it was automated in the sense that the stacks of paper were computer-printed documents instead of handwritten ones.

After that, the fidgeting CIO, whose eyes were darting around the room as he looked for an escape when we talked about software licenses, finally admitted that they were way behind in their renewals and way over on their usage. This was a substantial liability that would need to be cleaned up before any sale of the company.

A similar situation occurred when we were looking at acquiring a data center. In the discussion before our tour, we were told that all the data center doors were secured with electronic locks with fingerprint keypads. During the tour, sure enough, there were the keypads and the doors were unlocked by our host placing a hand on the keypads. There was also a big sign on one door advising, "Emergency Exit, Press Handle for 10 Seconds and Door Will Open." So much for the fingerprint-dependent security system.

Be aware of the perils of not listening. When we sold a business a couple years ago, the private equity company that was interested expressed concern on more than one occasion about our chairman, Boris, and his propensity to do all the talking. They wanted to hear from other members of the management team. I guess they were concerned that the rest of the management team was just stage props.

Our broker counseled us to speak more and Boris to speak much, much less. But Boris just couldn't help himself. At every meeting he would just talk. We had a presentation and each member of the team had a designated slot, but he would just take over and start talking. I tried to do my part by jumping in ahead of him and even interrupting and talking over him to let the potential buyers know that there was at least one other live body in the room. At one point, I even disagreed with Boris in the meeting, something my training had taught me never to do. But, we needed to demonstrate that we were free thinkers and not just props for Boris.

I don't know if any of that helped, but we did consummate the sale. The sad fact is that we don't know how many of the other 10 or so companies that took a look as us walked away because of that same issue.

As mentioned previously, not only can you listen with your ears, you can listen with your eyes. "Reading" body language is critical to understanding what someone is thinking or even saying. Very few people are great poker players. It's not that we don't understand math and the odds of a 52-card deck. It's that we have "tells," little signals we subconsciously send about what's truly going on in our heads. Being alert to those will help you tremendously to understand.

During larger group meetings, many of the folks opposing whatever it is you're proposing aren't going to come straight at you. Those who are supportive or genuinely open and curious are the ones most likely to talk. Someone who's against you will save their powder for some one-on-one discussions with the decision maker. You need to recognize these people and try to engage them, even ask them what they think. They won't lie and say they're in love with something they're not. They may not come right out with their complaints, but you'll get some idea of what's on their mind.

As you have these discussions and listen to the criticism, even from your friends, remember this is business. Accept the input and seek to make your proposal or project better. If you disagree, sharpen your arguments to demonstrate why your way is the correct way. Don't get angry, don't go into hiding, and don't ignore the criticisms. Address things head-on professionally and keep selling. If you lose, hold your head high from having fought the good fight, learn what works and what doesn't in your organization and vow to do better the next time. If you win, follow through.

The art of being a good listener is sadly underrated in business, where outbound communication is dominant. But, if you can master the skill of listening and couple it with decent other communications skills, you'll be highly effective in what you want to achieve.

In conclusion:
a. You learn by listening to others.
b. You don't learn by listening only to yourself.
c. If you're known as a listener, your words will have more impact when you do speak because they'll be more fact-based.
d. Listen with all your senses.
e. When you do speak, speak with passion not emotion.

Conversation 5 – It Isn't Personal and You're Going to Need a Cold Heart

Over my career, for the most part, I've had the good fortune to work with good people and have had an enjoyable experience while making a living. But, sometimes even the good folks buckle under pressure and lash out. And, as the world is not solely populated by good people, there are a number of asses you'll run into and the asses do what asses do. Now, the people who like to yell are one type you'll have to have a thick skin against. But there's another type, those who belittle and make snide remarks, coming in with their agenda. They don't seek first to understand, and proceed to judge everyone guilty without benefit of a trial. This is probably a worse type of person than the yeller.

Let me add that some of the things I had to deal with and accept are things you hopefully won't encounter. Our personal interactions at the office have come under a lot more scrutiny and things that were accepted in my early career are way out of bounds now. However, just in case you hit a rough spot, a little insight from my experience.

You'll also need a thick skin when it comes to handling criticism, or, as it's often referred to, constructive criticism. You can dress it up with a nice adjective, but you're still going to want to have a thick skin. Nobody has ever written a presentation, report, memo or letter that their boss didn't find something wrong with. It's just the way people think.

I know I'm guilty of having to make some word change or structure change to things presented to me. Not because the work was bad, just that I saw a way to make it better. As you go through your career, you have to accept that others will see things slightly or evenly dramatically differently than you do. You need to accept their input, listen to what they say, and adjust your approach, words, etc. Taking it personally, or being so in love with the work that you can't accept input or new ideas, will lead to nothing but distress.

However, if after listening carefully to the proposed change and reasons given you feel they are not understanding the points you made, then by all means speak up. But argue with facts and logic, not emotion. "We/I worked so hard on this" will not cause the boss to forget their own ideas and say, "By all means, submit this crappy work." But, if the boss is wrong, make them see the light.

Similarly, when it comes time for a personnel appraisal, don't be surprised when you're not rated a rock star in every category. And, please don't be shocked when they don't back up whatever score they gave you with the 10 reasons and 33 sub-reasons of things you didn't do or did poorly to justify the average score. They don't have detailed reasons; they just know you didn't wow them related to that line item on the appraisal. The important thing to remember is to avoid any "needs improvements." If you have one of those, definitely try to find out what caused them to mark you down there. Otherwise hope for all "averages" with an occasional "rock star" rating on a couple of areas.

Conversely, if you have a boss who does rate you as a rock star across the board, be happy, but make sure you have someone else as your mentor and consider trying to transfer to a different area to get a new boss. That's because the boss you have isn't giving you honest feedback -- they just want to avoid controversy. You won't learn much from them.

Hmm, this sounds pretty miserable.

That's why they invented happy hour.

Now, along with having a thick skin, you have to remember it's not personal, you will be called on to do things you really would rather not do, things that you might not necessarily agree with. I'm not talking about illegal things. Nobody's going to ask you to kill anyone or run drugs across the border. I'm talking about general business activities and personnel management actions that you will have to take that will cause someone else to have a very bad day. To accomplish these activities successfully and maintain your own mental health, you're going to need a little bit of a cold heart.

As soon as you gain any supervisory responsibility or have client management responsibilities, you will start hearing very touching stories about why something wasn't done, can't be done, can't be paid for, etc. Some of those stories might even be true. So what if they are? Can you afford to pay people for not working? Can you give away your products or services because your customer is having some financial difficulties? The answers should be no. If they're not, then soon you'll be the one telling the sad stories.

What you need to do is listen (there's that word again) to the story, understand the root cause, and then work with the employee or client or supplier on a solution that allows you to achieve what you need while they are able to address whatever is causing them to not perform in the first place.

Maybe it's changing the employee's hours or allowing them to temporarily work from home. For clients, maybe it's slowing down projects or providing them agreed-to short-term financing at market rates reflective of their situation. Whatever it is, the goal should be to keep your business whole first, and then provide them with some relief if possible.

Another area where tough skin and cold hearts are helpful is when the dreaded layoffs are announced. Now the accepted statement is "nobody likes layoffs," please repeat. Honestly, while I wish that were true, I believe there's a small group of sick bastards that enjoys them, inflicting suffering on innocent people to please the investment world or meet company targets of some sort.

So, if you're like me and find having to lay someone off a sickening exercise, you're going to have to put on your thickest skin, drink the coldest ice water you can find and harden both mind and body to the task. Afterwards, I find a good whiskey helps.

For those of you who have not ever gone through the process, let's say it can be a little random. You might assume that the lower performers might go first, but that might not be possible since for some positions there's only one person filling it and you need that work to continue. You also have to manage EEOC compliance and make sure the final group selected doesn't disproportionally affect any protected group. And lastly, if you just happen to have the misfortune to be on the shit list of anyone contributing names to the layoff list, watch out.

After the list is created, it normally falls to the frontline managers to deliver the bad news to the folks affected on their team. I've had to do this a few times and, in a word, it sucks.

To make my points in this Conversation, I do need to provide fair warning that the language may get a little blue.

Illustrative Cases:

When is a thick skin called for? To illustrate, let me describe a meeting I once participated in where the subject of a centralized IT help desk came up. There was a substantive group of directors, vice presidents and even the senior vice president/controller in the meeting at the shared services center (SSC). One of the topics brought up by the head of the SSC was his desire to have his own IT help desk instead of relying on the help desk that serviced the rest of the company. As the discussion progressed and I continued to make the case for the status quo, I could see the steam coming out of the SSC head's ears.

Now, I had worked with him for over two years and knew he could be an ass, but we had always maintained a level of professionalism. Not this day.

After I met his unsubstantiated demand that we set up a separate help desk with another try at explaining the logic of a centralized one –

economies of scale, consistency of service, the fact that IT personnel usually got involved as all but the simplest questions got escalated to level 2 or 3, and the practical fact he had no place to put one – he suddenly went off. "What the fuck happens, you move into IT they open up your head pour shit in and stir it around!?!" he bellowed.

Strong words, but I just calmly replied, "No." He then slammed his chair back from the table, stormed out of the room and locked himself in his office. He was relieved of command a short time after, and shortly after that, let go. I, on the other hand, moved on and up.

In that situation, a business meeting, I didn't think then, nor do I think now, that doing a throw down and demanding apologies or talking about hostile work environments would have done me any favors. I knew he had just killed his own career and my going crazy and losing my cool in response would only have killed mine. Take the hit, have that thick skin, and let the insults just pass you by.

Big businesses don't like controversy. If you find yourself in a situation where you might have every right to strike back, think twice. Just because you're in the right doesn't make it right.

In the meantime, if you're ever in Alpharetta, Georgia and drive by the Ryder SSC, if you listen closely you can still hear the f-bombs reverberating through the pines.

In another situation, I was discussing with the client VP an upcoming rollout of some application software changes. The client was a consumer lending company with branch offices across the country. At the time, telecommunication costs were high so we had built them a system that ran on individual AS/400 computers in each office. This configuration gave us the ability to be a little more cautious in our rollout. While the updates had been tested, there was still a chance some issues might be uncovered in real-world usage.

With that in mind, I proposed a short pilot period at a few sites. Now as there was no pending drop-dead date like Y2K that we were dealing with, the cost of the pilot was essentially zero. Moreover, as a practical matter, all sites couldn't get the new release on the same day anyway. I was a bit surprised when the VP refused. Thinking I perhaps hadn't explained clearly, I tried again. My attempt to re-explain was met with a fusillade of "Fuck you, fuck fuck fuck!" To this day, I have no idea why he went ballistic. We could have simply agreed to disagree and moved on. Which, as he was the client and it was his system, we did. I documented our position in the status report and other management documents and left him to do as he wanted.

The application changes worked, which was good news. But, good luck does not substitute for good planning. The changes could just as easily have had a bug and we'd have been facing a major cleanup effort.

Later the partner I was working for approached me about the encounter. I guess the client had brought it up to him in some roundabout way and said he was just trying to educate me. Interesting, I already knew how to say "fuck."

Does this stuff still really go on?

These first two stories are a little to the extreme side of things, but, yes, it does happen. Maybe fewer f-bombs, but the yelling, sure. In my case, the two stories are 100% accurate, only maybe louder in reality. Hopefully for younger folks, this doesn't happen at all, but even if nobody's tossing f-bombs, there are more subtle ways to try to demean and embarrass subordinates and opponents.

Over time, I admit I have developed a different approach to handling these things. If someone starts to raise their voice and rant at me, I tell them "Look, I can yell and swear just as loud as you. But, that's not going to get us anywhere. Do you want to discuss this or not?"

If they keep ranting, I simply leave. All but one time this strategy has worked. They come around an hour or a day later, apologize, and we get on with business. The one time it didn't work, they sent someone to counsel me that while the other person had been wrong, I shouldn't have walked out. I respectfully disagreed. While having a thick skin means not breaking down under assault or criticism, it doesn't mean blind acceptance of the unacceptable.

As mentioned, it's not only yelling you'll need to be ready for, there's also weird psychological games and yes abuse. When we were working on a project to select new financial, distribution, and manufacturing software for a national juice company, we had a situation that brought a difficult individual into our lives. I was a brand-new manager tasked with leading the financial and distribution team. Another manager had the manufacturing team, with both of us reporting to the same senior manager and partner.

During the course of the project, the senior manager went out on maternity leave and the partner had to drop out for back surgery. To replace them, the Firm brought in two partners from Chicago. The lead partner was an old guy, Dennis; the other was a new partner, Dianne.

Within a few days their arrival, it was clear that Dennis had an agenda and Dianne was there primarily to do project management activities while Dennis worked his scheme. Neither of them had much interest in knowing what we were all working on or how we had got to where we were.

Dennis's first objective was to clean house. For some inexplicable reason, to begin that he set his eyes on Nick, a staff consultant working for me. Now Nick was a likeable guy, quiet, but dedicated to his work and trying to do the right thing each day. The client liked him and nobody was complaining.

But Dennis decided he had to go. Rather than face Nick while he was in the office, Dennis waited until Friday, and then called me from the airport and told me to get rid of Nick. I said "Okay, we'll work out a transition plan and figure out when we can make that happen."

He said "No, you don't understand, I want him gone now! Today!" Okay...

Another manager (who Nick was also working for) and I then took Nick to lunch. As we sat down at TGI Fridays, she and I simultaneously said, "Nick, today's your last day, pack your things when we get back." We both then proceeded to order cocktails while Nick looked at us with a very puzzled face.

When we got back to the office, the client was just as puzzled. And, being the nice folks they were, hastily arranged a farewell party. The Firm looked stupid that afternoon.

But, Dennis wasn't done. He then set his Chicago minions loose to harass, harangue, and chastise other members of the team. I actually had to go talk one guy down who was so upset he was crying in the men's room. Picture that, an adult man so upset by the verbal abuse he's getting from management that he's reduced to crying in a restroom stall. And there I am in the stall next door trying to calm him down. Just writing this makes me a little pissed again.

Dennis's next kindergarten-style attack came when he forced the client to tear down the cubicle walls that surrounded my desk and two other managers' desks. None of us had asked for the semi-private spaces and we hadn't built the damn things, we just sat where we were told to sit. But Dennis looked at it as a way to embarrass us and I guess to show he was the big boss.

This pattern continued for weeks. Petty attacks, the singling out of a staff person, isolating them from the herd and then pouncing like a hyena on the poor person with final acts of humiliation and assault before unceremoniously dismissing them from the project.

After spending lots of political capital and dozens of calls, I was finally able to orchestrate my own exit off this fun house project. Dennis and his henchmen and henchwomen could have the damn place.

Throughout this ugly period, I couldn't understand what Dennis's problem was. I was in agreement with the software direction he wanted to go with. In fact, I had given a presentation to the client supporting that direction before Dennis got there. But that direction was overruled by the partner in charge at that time. The only answer then was to soldier on and find a way out. In today's world, lawsuits would fly.

Yikes, I'm starting to think about just staying in school.

I understand that -- it's nice, but it doesn't pay as well. Again, the stoires I'm including are outliers, but they can happen and you have to be ready to get through the situation and safely out the other side.

At Ryder we went through reorganizations on a somewhat regular basis. Each time I was told who had to go, and regardless of whether I agreed or not, I had to execute.

You can't explain to the individual why because there is no explanation. You can't offer much humanity either, because to avoid lawsuits the process is highly scripted. It's "you're being separated, if you sign this waiver you'll receive this package, Terry will help you pack your things now."

While you're having that conversation, IT has shut off the employee's systems access, their key card has been deactivated, parking space painted over and someone has dropped some empty boxes in their office or cubicle where a member of the security team now stands to watch them pack. Then they can do the walk past all their former coworkers carrying their boxes and that ugly lamp they had.

I remember one time when we did layoffs it seemed like every secretary in the company was on the list. The first one I did was a single woman who took the news calmly and then said, "Well, better me than Pat since she has her kids to care for." You can probably guess who was next on the list I'd been given: Pat.

But, worse even than letting the single mother go, was when I had to lay off another employee who was in cancer treatment.

Whoa, aren't cancer patients protected?

Well yes, they are, by the Americans with Disabilities Act (ADA). But like all protected classes, when it comes to layoffs, it's not that you can't lay them off, it's that you can't discriminate against them. You can't single out people of a protected class such as only lay off people with cancer or lay off a disproportionate percentage of people with disabilities vs. those in other groups. Human resources creates the list very carefully and that's why sometimes someone who *should* go based on performance doesn't go. Regardless, every time you have the layoff conversation, you're going to find you've got to have a cold heart.

As I said at the beginning of this conversation, I've been fortunate in terms of the people I've worked for and with. With a couple exceptions, they were all good folks. Hopefully you will have equal or better luck. Regardless of whether anybody ever curses at you or asks the makeup of your brain, at a minimum you will face constructive criticism and the need to deliver very bad news. How you handle yourself in those situations is critical. You can't break down, be defensive, be unnecessary mean or too understanding. You need to play it straight down the middle – "Eye of the Tiger" and all that. In case you don't recognize the song reference, it's from the 1982 film Rocky, starring Sylvestor Stallone. If you haven't seen it, find it on one of the streaming services, good film.

In conclusion:
   a. You have to have a tough skin to handle attacks on and criticism of your work.
   b. You will need to deliver very bad news in a professional manner, without emotion.
   c. Don't become so attached to your own work product that you can't accept constructive criticism.

Conversation 6 — Use Your Experts

I've been a consultant and hired a lot of consultants over the years. One thing that still amazes me is how someone will hire consultants to help them accomplish something, and then proceed to tell the consultants how to do their work and to ignore all the advice and guidance the consultant provides. To me that's just crazy.

You may see people discuss things with the outside legal counsel or their accountants, but you won't see them ignore their advice. No, those professionals are listened to. Same with doctors. People will seek second opinions, maybe, but the "I hired you for your expertise, now do what I say" doesn't happen with anyone else but business consultants. Weird.

When you hire an expert consultant, along with bringing in people, you are bringing in foreign processes and approaches. While the expert is there, try to learn about their approach, If they're getting things done you couldn't on your own, some of that may be due to their approach. Adopting it into your own organization or personal tool box can provide some additional value after the expert is gone.

The point of this is that during your career you'll often either find yourself working alongside people from outside consulting firms or you'll be hiring them yourself. Either way, take advantage of the situation to learn from them and, most importantly, to listen to what they have to say. They aren't perfect, but if you or others thought enough of their credentials and experience to hire them and pay their rates, they're worth a hearing.

Illustrative Cases:

My story in Conversation 3 about the accounts receivable (AR) system where the client ignored our advice and the results were a disaster is an example of this behavior. In that case, the CEO doubled down in that after he ignored our advice, he then proceeded to blame us for not giving him better advice for getting out of the ditch he had driven into. What an asshole. Sorry, some people just are and he fits the mold.

On a more positive note, my experience with KPMG while working at Ryder is more demonstrative of how to better work with consultants. Ryder was using KPMG on a number of projects plus they were the company's auditors (this was before Enron and some of the restrictions on accounting firms and what they could do for a company if they were the auditors).

As it came time to replace payroll for Y2K and other reasons, we were faced with needing to get things done by a certain date at the most reasonable cost possible. Since we were also working with Accenture at the time, we felt it appropriate to solicit bids from both parties, Accenture and KPMG. Each one proposed but only KPMG was willing to commit to getting the project done on time and for a fixed fee. Accenture's plan took us well into 2000, was about 50% more costly, and was not a fixed fee. Given the timing, we also would have to add remediation of the existing system or a temporary switch to an outside provider, all at even more additional cost.

As I mentioned, we had worked with KPMG successfully in the past, liked their proposed team, and they were our auditors so we felt they would be unlikely to leave us hanging. We selected KPMG.

While all of these projects were going on, we had entered into an alliance with Accenture and IBM. Accenture would handle applications development and support and IBM would handle technology infrastructure including network, server/mainframe, and help desk. Accenture was the lead, as they told us practically every day, but IBM had the lion's share of the fees.

As the alliance got rolling, there were some normal hiccups and learning to work together moments. All parties involved made their share of mistakes. But the one thing I could always depend on IBM to do was to eventually complete whatever was asked for or that they tasked themselves with. It might not be done as fast as I wanted -- in fact it seldom was -- but it would get done correctly and we would eventually gain the benefits.

IBM was responsible for our communications network. There were a lot of parts to that and with 842 branch operations plus a handful of other major installations, there was plenty of room for issues to arise.

However, on their own initiative, IBM took up the task of addressing each part of the network, replacing switches and wiring as needed, upgrading equipment, and making other modifications to improve the performance and reliability of the network. They weren't doing this out of kindness; the better the network was, the less labor it took them to keep it going. From my seat though, it was sure nice to have some professionals recognize a win/win and take action to achieve it.

My last story of how not to treat experts is more recent. One of the programs I introduced at Clinical was an annual mock inspection. We would hire a former Food and Drug Administration (FDA) inspector and have them conduct a mock inspection of one of our large projects. This would have several benefits. It would validate that our quality management system was sufficient, gave us an early look at a significant project so we could fix things before any real FDA inspection, and provided training for our staff on what FDA inspectors look for and how to interact with them.

We tried to make it as real as possible, with the person we hired staying in character. We had done two of these mock inspections and each one had found issues which resulted in updates to processes, training and certainly project files.

When we did the third one in 2019, the operations team lost their minds. The inspector was one we had used before but was not our first choice. Regardless, she knew her stuff although she was maybe a little brusque in her questioning. Then again, you don't get to pick your real FDA inspector so having a tough mock inspection is good, because it gets you ready for anything.

Unfortunately, operations saw the whole process as an assault on them. And, instead of looking at it as the learning exercise it was, they crawled into their bunker and started lobbing hand grenades out at the inspector and me.

Nothing the inspector found was incorrect; operations just didn't like being told they weren't superstars. Well, sorry, guys, you weren't. They were blaming quality assurance, the inspector, everyone but themselves for some major and critical findings, and missing the entire point of the exercise. Instead of learning, they erected walls and set out to destroy those on the other side. Sad, sad, sad. But it's a good demonstration of how people can sometimes react negatively when the outside expert holds up the mirror.

In conclusion:
    a. Listen to the experts that you hire (or are hired by others but who you work with).
    b. Learn from their experience.
    c. Consider adopting some of the experts' processes and approaches yourself.

Conversation 7 – Ask and Ye Shall Receive

One thing in business is that everything is negotiable. The corollary is if you don't ask, nobody is going to offer. My experience has shown that some folks are just averse to negotiating; they get a quote for something or an offer made to them and they take it at face value, making their decision without once asking for something better. Some find negotiating unseemly, while others feel the other side will say "no," so why bother.

Well, it's business, and if you think negotiating is unseemly, I think you seriously need to consider a different career path. And unless you're a mind reader, how do you know what the other guy will say if asked? He might be under tremendous pressure to get your business, and even if the price can't move maybe other terms and conditions can be made more advantageous. The point is: *Ask*.

Now I'm not advising that you try to squeeze a nickel and make Jefferson cry. No, I'm a firm believer in win/win. But, it's nice if the home team maybe wins just a little more, and certainly not less. In any transaction there are many moving parts, so find the ones that really matter and ask for something better.

But wouldn't it be better if everyone just offered the best deal to start with?

Interesting question. It would be if there was such a thing as the best deal. What's best for you might not be what's best for me. A supplier isn't going to know what we want, what we need or what we consider best unless we say something. Again, you have to ask.

Illustrative Cases:

Let me offer a couple stories. First up: a somewhat humorous and simple-to-understand life lesson. While still living in Tampa and working for Arthur Andersen, I was assigned to a project in Miami. Back then we typically flew to our out-of-town assignments late Sunday or early Monday and then home late Friday afternoon. On the Tampa-Miami route we flew Eastern Airlines, which flew Boeing 727s with two classes of service, coach and first. They also had a frequent flyer program that allowed you to get upgraded to first class if it was available, first come, first served at the gate.

Now it might not sound like it's worthwhile to get an upgrade for a 30-minute flight, but after a long week, any perk sounds good. And if you hurried, you could get three drinks, one on the ground and two in the air.

So, on one Friday, my team of other three people from Tampa and I did our Friday afternoon run to the Miami airport and then to the gate. When we got there, I walked up and requested the upgrades for us. The gate agent was polite but said she didn't think they could accommodate us as they were fully booked. She suggested taking our assigned seats in coach. I thanked her, but with a smile said that if anything changed to please not forget about us.

Shortly after that, we boarded.

Just as we were sitting down in our assigned coach seats, a flight attendant came up to me and said, "Mr. Urban, can you please come forward with the rest of your party?" (I'd never had a party before: I guess today they would have said my posse.) We grabbed our bags and went forward where four nice wide seats awaited us.

While that would have made for a nice trip any week, this particular week it was a godsend. The plane had some minor technical issue and we didn't take off for three more hours. During that time, they opened the first class bar and we drank, talked and laughed. We enjoyed ourselves with some folks who worked for Burdines (now Macy's) and were also returning home.

After about two hours they started allowing coach passengers to get off the plane for food and such. They were some glum-looking people. I suppose the empty bottles, party hats and streamers in first class didn't make them any happier. Had I not made the extra request to the agent not to forget us, we likely would have been among those folks.

But those seats were empty, surely they would have remembered you when they saw that?

Not necessarily, though undoubtedly they would have put somebody in those seats. But just as likely it would have been four frequent flyers who walked up after us or were waiting on standby. The ground crew's focus was getting the plane loaded and out of there. Any solution was easier than the one they chose, having me and my party change seats. No, I'm convinced it was me asking to not be forgotten -- and my smiling baby-blue eyes.

Now, back to the business of negotiation. While I was at Ryder and we were building out the shared services center (SSC), one of the things we had to do was consolidate the AS/400's. Now technically this was not a huge problem. There were large AS/400's we could get that could easily carry the load from the multiple smaller ones we had. The problem was finance, specifically the book value the AS/400s had as an asset on our books. We had to find a way to get rid of them and replace them without taking a book loss on the disposition of the assets.

What to do? The thing to do was to ask the provider of AS/400s, IBM.

We gave the IBM representative on site the situation (she was already familiar as she tracked us closely), did a little feint that we might need to port the system to HP if they couldn't help us, and then left them to work on the issue. As expected, they came back with a very attractive financial deal to allow us to swap our 100 small AS/400's for 9 larger ones, with a goal of reducing the 9 down to 7. We swooped in to grab the deal and got rid of the albatross of over-valued assets.

Similarly, more recently when we had to move because our lease was ending and we needed more space at Clinical, we were faced with the issue of not being able to fully complete our move before the end of the lease. Again, we didn't sit, I asked the landlord. He said sure. It did take more than one follow-up call to get him to execute. I think he was just distracted not malicious, but we got the open ended extension we wanted with no commitment to a minimum number of months on our part.

Here's a very recent story. When business conditions and a new CEO brought large layoffs to my last employer, I got caught in the net.

One of the issue I was concerned with were the stock options I held. When we had sold the business two years prior, 30% of the value I was to receive had to be put back into the business. For tax reasons this was done in the form of "rollover" stock options.

Now these options represented a significant sum and I didn't want, nor did I feel it was right, to just to walk away from them. The option grants allowed for 90 days post-employment to exercise options. However, this would again lead to a tax issue, namely that I'd owe tax on the difference between the strike price and the real value of the options, even though I would be receiving no cash.

So, what to do? Leave the options? Not good and really not fair, since I wasn't being dismissed for cause, just poor sales -- which was somebody else's job. Exercise the options and pay the tax? Also not good, we were talking a stiff tax bill. Option 3? Well, that had to be found. So, I asked the board of directors, "What can we do?"

I presented a couple options and they came back with a third that satisfied my needs. They didn't have to do anything and if I hadn't asked they wouldn't' have volunteered. But when I asked, they saw the issue and recognized that there was a need to find an equitable solution, which they did. Had I not asked, had I just sat and gotten pissed off or threatened to sue, I'm confident I would not have reached the deal I did with them. As it is, I got want

I wanted given the circumstances and we're all still on good terms.

A little happier scenario that involved asking/negotiation was my path to vice president at Ryder. As mentioned in the introduction, I started out as a group manager, then after a year I was a director, and after two more years I was a senior director. At that point that I was put in charge of all IT for the leasing division and corporate. We were moving into the alliance with Accenture and IBM, but somebody had to be in charge of things from Ryder's point of view.

I had a very small staff but all the responsibility. And as it turns out, all meant *all*. Nothing moved as it related to Ryder Transportation Services (RTS) IT without getting my blessing. This wasn't necessarily my idea, but it was what we had to do in order to maintain some control and get something done. Otherwise, the alliance would spend all its time, and our money, making life nicer for themselves, particularly Accenture.

After demonstrating I could keep the ship of state sailing, was loyal to Ryder, could prudently improve the cost value equation, and was a team player, I decided I deserved more. The next organizational step was group director. But, I didn't like the sound of that and felt it did not fairly reflect the position I held. Previous people who had my job were all given the title of vice president, the only difference being that while they had employees to do things, I had the alliance. Employees would have been easier, because you could command them, while I had to cajole, beg, threaten, and negotiate everything.

Taking my own advice, I asked the Jim, the division president and my boss, for a promotion to VP. Jim thought about it for a while. This was not a trivial request, as we weren't a bank but a Fortune 500 company. After a few weeks, Jim came through for me. As a nice added touch, he made the announcement in public when the alliance and my team had gathered to cut the cake celebrating my fortieth birthday. A nice birthday present. Thanks Jim.

In conclusion:
a. You have to ask in order to get.
b. Be bold in what you ask for; you'll be surprised how much you might actually get.
c. The worst effect from asking is that they say "no."

Conversation 8 – Dealing With Naysayers

Any major initiative (and some small ones) you undertake in business will attract more than its fair share of naysayers, those people who apparently have extra time to come by and tell you all the issues you'll face or, better yet, mutter it to others. You know the type, they always have a half-grin, half-grimace of their face as they point out the flaws in every idea, program, or project. Some will be minor annoyances, like Bob (who I mentioned in the introduction), and others will be lethal killers, like AH discussed later in this Conversation. You'll need to deal with both kinds.

The bigger the effort is, the more of these folks will come along. They're worse than the people who bet on the "Don't Pass" line in craps. At least those folks are betting with the house. No, the naysayers don't want anyone to succeed. You, the business, the guy/gal down the street, anyone. They seem to thrive in a world of universal misery.

But, if you're going to succeed in business, you've got to take them on. And the best way to do that is to hit them with facts. Overwhelm them with data, plans, whatever you've got handy. One thing naysayers like is to BS, and analyzing facts gets too close to real work for them.

If they still keep coming, tell them whatever issue they're talking about is covered in some document – pick whatever one is most voluminous and dense. They'll never check. And, if they do, well, by then you could have added something and then tell them you're sorry you got the reference wrong.

Now, did I just tell you to lie? No, not exactly. Whatever ticky-tack point they're trying to make is most likely covered in your plans and designs. But you don't have time to go dig it out to satisfy their random mumblings. If they want to look, God bless. And if they happened to have stumbled on a valid point, well, updating the books is just a little creative project management.

The point is, they're like a cancer: you can't just ignore them and you sure don't want them around. They will wear on you and worse, on whoever is above you with the power to kill the project. You've got to neutralize them. Often they'll be long-term employees and maybe even hold a senior title. Regardless, make sure you keep control of the narrative and keep them distracted with so much data they can't possibly consume it, let alone understand it. They'll soon grow tired of coming after your initiative and go bother someone else.

Why not just try to take them out, discredit them, and take them on head-on? First, due to seniority or who knows what, there's a reason they're still walking the halls. Everyone knows what they are but there they stand. Second, on occasion, while their delivery bites, they may have a kernel of insight that's useful. You just have to dig through a pile of crap to get it.

Illustrative Cases:

Back in Conversation 6, I mentioned the payroll replacement project at Ryder. To recap, we had to do something with payroll for Y2K reasons, plus it was just an out-of-date system prone to error. We ended up going with KPMG and installing SAP. Competing for the consulting business was Accenture, who we had an "alliance" with for support of our business applications.

Multiple times, I made an effort to explain the situation to the Accenture partner. We had an old, error-prone payroll system that was not worth remediating for Y2K. We were only putting in payroll functionality of SAP, not the entire HR suite. We had used and trusted KPMG before, and very senior executives way higher than me were behind this., Finally, payroll was a very small department and there were no plans to change anything in the overall process or pay methods that would impact the Ryder employees. My hope was they would see the light and come back with a lower bid. And, even after their bid kept coming in higher, defending them to Ryder management with an explanation that they were not trying to shaft us, rather they just had a different approach. Which they did – a hell of lot of money for change management, which was overkill for a 10-person department.

After awarding the project to KPMG, the Accenture partner went on a jihad to sink the project and get everyone responsible fired. I guess he hadn't read my Conversation on having a thick skin and not taking it personally. He made if very personal.

But, we beat him back with facts. First of all, we had to do something; that wasn't in doubt. Second, we had a fixed bid from a reputable firm (KPMG was the company's auditors and had successfully implemented the new accounting systems). Third, we had full support of all the Ryder executives from the affected areas. And, lastly we had a fixed, controllable scope. All the partner had were scare tactics and bitching. He lost, the project went forward, and the system was still running more than 15 years later when I was last there.

While we were implementing the solution, I got a hopeful sign of people's willingness to change one day in the cafeteria. As I stood in line, I overheard one of the young ladies in front of me say to another, "As soon as I learn this new SAP stuff, I'm outta here."

As an executive of the company, I should have been horrified to hear an employee so unhappy working there. But as the guy responsible for getting SAP in, I was thrilled. I knew I would have at least one very attentive, enthusiastic participant on the team.

In conclusion, to deal with naysayers:

    a. Don't fight by their rules, they can only win if you do.

    b. They're fact-averse, so spray them with data.

    c. They tire easily, weather the storm.

Conversation 9 – Trust Yourself

After listening, I believe that having trust in one's self is the second-most important business skill. With good listening skills you'll be informed, have insights others don't, and will have facts upon which to make decisions. But, to make those decisions, you also have to trust yourself.

As you go through your career, and hopefully find yourself moving up through the management ranks, you'll find that you have fewer and fewer people inside the company you can ask for advice or help. You can certainly ask your subordinates and peers for input, but as you reach the top levels of the business, even those are fewer in number. And, even with input, you ultimately will be called on to make the decision. Something that some folks, no matter how smart, are just incapable of doing.

Decisions are tough, you put yourself at risk every time you make one. If something goes wrong, who gets blamed? You. So what do you do?

My experience has taught me that after soliciting input, internal and external, in the end you have to trust your gut. You are your own best friend, you have no ulterior motives except your success, so advice you give yourself is apolitical and untainted. If you've done the due diligence and align that with what your gut (your experience) tells you is the right answer, you'll tend to make good decisions.

But what about my own biases, won't they interfere with me making an objective decision?

Very good question. We all have internal biases. The due diligence that you need to do before making any decision has got to account for that bias. But once the due diligence is done and the analysis complete, if there's no clear winner, avoid the temptation to redo the analysis. I have developed a theorem I call Gary's Law of Constant Numbers (it's discussed in the Useful Hints conversation). Now this law mostly applies to estimating things, but it still holds true for any sort of comparative analysis. Simply stated, the more you redo an estimate, the more you'll keep coming back to essentially the same answer. You can modify your assumptions and factors and whatever else you're using, but in the end you'll be back where you started.

What accounts for this? Internal bias. So, what should you do? Stop. A couple passes through the estimating model, or in this case, the analysis, is enough. If it's not giving you a clear answer, it's time to do something else. In the case of estimates, accept the estimate and make your decision accordingly. In the case of making a decision based on a broader analysis, trust you gut and decide.

Now someone might second guess you and (particularly after time has passed and situations have changed) make fun of historical decisions. But in the moment, when the call has to be made, you'll do the right thing listening to your gut. Remember, standing still is not an option; you must move. Be the leader, make the decision, set the goal and move forward. Don't look back.

Damn, this sounds like a lot of responsibility, what if I'm wrong?

If you've done your homework, thought through the issue logically, not emotionally, you'll find you make more right decisions than wrong ones. If you did make a wrong decision, recognize it, own it, and take action to find that safe exit and minimize any negative results. The only people who don't make wrong decisions in business are those who make no decisions. Just don't make a habit of it.

Illustrative Cases:

Here's a story of trusting my gut from the very beginning of my career. As part of its training program, Arthur Andersen had all new Management Information Consulting Division (MICD) personnel attend a three-week programming course at their training center in St. Charles, Illinois.

During the training, we would work 8-5, break until 7 and then work 7-10, Monday through Friday. Saturdays and Sundays were lighter 8-hour days. Other than the class work and eating, about the only activity in those early years was two hours of drinking at the bar in the basement from 10 to midnight. As I recall, they did seem to have an endless supply of pretzels and goldfish crackers at the bar. High class.

The work itself was demanding for those of us with nontechnical, nonprogramming backgrounds. We were tasked with writing several programs in a very limited amount of time. The objective was to teach us not only the basics of COBOL programming, but also hard work, long hours, tight timelines and stress management. As the weeks progressed, I actually found myself dreaming about my program and looking at everything from a COBOL code, step-by-step perspective.

Weird rules were put in place to make it even harder. Until you got a clean compile, all of your code had to be keypunched on cards. No White-Out, so if you made a typing mistake, type a new card. You then had to manage a big stack of these things to keep them in the proper order as you made changes to the program.

With your stack of cards, you were only allowed three runs on the mainframe per day. This was to get us used to being frugal with, at the time, the limited computing power available at our clients. Finally, after a clean compile you could use the online editor, but were still limited to the three runs.

During the class, both as a student and years later as an instructor, I saw more than one person stumble and break under the pressure.

In order get through the training program, you had to be bright, organized and able to manage your time. You also had to be able to dig deep inside yourself and recognize that you had it in you to get this done in spite of never seeing it before and being forced to drink from the proverbial fire hose. Belief in myself was key to getting through it and the cornerstone of the confidence I would need to regularly walk into new situations with new clients and act like I knew something while frantically consuming all the information I could. The duck on the pond comes to mind, calm and serene on the surface, paddling like hell under the water.

Now the previous story might just have been youthful exuberance. After all, the Firm wouldn't have hired me to see me fail. But this next story deals with a real business situation with significant impact to the business if I got it wrong. It was also a situation where I was truly alone. No one else in the business could make the decision, and no one could even offer much advice. It was mid-career when I had to make the call to replace the communication network for Ryder's 842 branches. When I started at Ryder, the branches communicated on a network of shared 9.6K lines that routed back to district offices where branch systems ran on AS/400s in the district office. From there the network went over a series of factional T1s back to headquarters (HQ) and the mainframe. This was called the "Spider Network," probably a misnomer because spider webs are actually more structured and organized than this thing was.

In the introduction, I mentioned that one of the first projects at Ryder was to set up the shared services center (SSC), which took the AS/400s out of the district offices. To keep the Spider Network working and not spend a fortune, we took the path of least resistance and left a switch in each district office to relay the network back to HQ, where we had series of T1 connections to Atlanta and the SSC. While this solution worked, it was far from optimal. The network was slow, could not handle high-volume traffic needs, was unreliable, and was very difficult to diagnose since there were so many parts and outside vendors involved.

While I was doing my thing with the SSC, there was another team working on replacing the branch systems. They too didn't like the Spider Network and investigated options, but could get no one responsible to make a decision to change.

After some significant corporate restructuring, I found myself in charge of all IT for the Ryder leasing division (RTS) and system support for corporate. This included the SSC and the branch operations as well as all the infrastructure they ran on the Spider Network. One of my first acts was to take a look at replacing this network.

After reviewing the options, this being 1997, it was clear to me there was only one viable solution, satellite. Cable internet was in its infancy. Some locations could get a DSL circuit through the phone company, but those were limited and prone to failure too.

The satellite solution was clean, put a small dish at each site communicating through the Hughes Satellite Network and from there to our SSC via T1 circuits. Our network cost would fall substantially, we could contract for 99.9999% availability, and any issues could more quickly be diagnosed since it would be a much simpler network with fewer players and links.

But, there was a lot of pushback from corners of IT not under my control. They kept trying to equate satellite to Direct TV and kept asking what happens when it rains or snows. They ignored the fact that I wasn't broadcasting the very large data packets TV requires and the dishes to be installed, while small, had at least four times the surface area of a Direct TV dish.

So, there I was, with a decision to make: Leave things alone or take the chance and change to get the cost and reliability benefits? After reviewing the facts again, driving around town seeing all the satellite dishes on the tops of gas stations, banks, and fast food restaurants, I went with my gut and said go.

The installation went quickly and smoothly. All the benefits were realized. The overall network system lasted until 2010 when cable internet connections became widely available at reasonable prices.

Let me give you another somewhat less dramatic decision, but one that at the time caused me great concern. I was a new staff member at AA, working on implementation of new financial systems at a small hospital. One of my tasks was to code a program to allocate certain costs by department and then create journal vouchers (JVs or transactions) to be posted by the system.

I started the task by reviewing the technical design specifications given to me that had been prepared by an AA senior manager. As I reviewed the design I observed that there seemed to be a flaw in it. Walking carefully through the design, it appeared to me that it was having the program create JVs after they had already been posted. This would mean these JVs would go nowhere and cost allocation wouldn't occur as planned.

If the Firm was one thing, it was hierarchical. A senior manager was several rungs up the ladder from me, so who was I to question their design? But, I knew my review was right and that surely nobody would want me to code a design that didn't work. So, I took my findings to the partner, a grumpy old guy also named Gary. We sat down in the small hospital cafeteria and he took both the design and the code I shared with him and started going through it himself, grunting as he did. It didn't take long until he announced, "You're right" and then made some quick changes to the design for me to work from. Big deal now, no, but as kid right out of school, it was then. And, it showed me early on the importance of trusting my gut.

That trust worked well for me later when I did a strategic planning effort for a fast food restaurant chain which had a brand that wasn't performing to plan. After reviewing a variety of data, including average check cost, locations, location demographics, marketing messaging, and sales per store, I came to a quick realization. They were positioning the brand as a high-quality product at a slightly higher price point than other competitors. The brand performed very well in upscale suburban markets and poorly in lower-income inner-city markets.

To me it was obvious: they were putting their stores in the wrong place. Since they were nowhere near saturating the more aligned demographic market, there were plenty of suburban and more affluent urban markets to put stores into. They had the added advantage of being able to convert the inner-city sites to the other brand in their portfolio which was more aligned to that demographic, thus avoiding any excess real estate issues.

When I first realized what the data was telling me, I thought, "This is too easy. Surely someone would have seen this." But, more data review didn't reveal anything else, so I went with my gut. They were surprised and thankful for the findings. How far they carried out the recommendations I don't know. New management came in shortly after I finished the project.

Much later in my career I needed to trust my gut in a very personal way. I had taken a position with Clinical, a contract research organization (CRO). Clinical's business was helping pharmaceutical and biotech companies plan, design and execute clinical trials to gain approval from regulators (the Food and Drug Administration, in the case of the US). My position was titled senior vice president process and quality, and I was to have the IT, quality assurance and training departments reporting to me. Later, I would take on talent acquisition to give it some needed leadership. The goal was to align all three organizations so that we had world-class compliance processes supported by custom technologies. At least, that was the chairman's (Boris) and my plan.

On my first day, as with any new job, I set out to meet the folks, starting with my own direct reports. The IT director was a young guy who definitely marched to his own drummer. But he was cordial and open about the state of the IT situation and I felt we'd get along fine. Training was only one nice young lady who was very enthusiastic but in over her head. Plus, the area was woefully underfunded and really a bit of a mess. Many, many hours and much debate would go into fixing this area.

My lead application developer for TALOS (which really only existed as a concept and some random code at this point in time) was remote. He was actually a young contract programmer in Macedonia. To this day I don't fully understand how he came to be, but he was nice enough and eager to build TALOS. He would just need direction on what that was and a push to deliver faster, completely and with good quality. We eventually got his visa issues fixed and he moved to the US. Interesting guy.

Quality Assurance (QA) was a whole different ball game.

Having been warned that the VP of QA was not necessarily a team player, I decided that as an act of respect I would go to his offices to meet instead of having him come to mine. When I sat down in his office the first thing out of his mouth was, "I won't report to you." Admittedly I was a little perplexed but I kept my cool and asked why. He then went on for several minutes (I learned this was one of his traits) talking about a variety of things. Everything from his offer letter, to independence, to White Sox baseball, and rooting out drunk employees. After he finished his soliloquy I thanked him for his time and said I'd be in touch.

After discussing the situation with Boris, we agreed that I would work with the QA VP (let's call him Frank), but at the appropriate time I'd let Boris know when we could make a change. Going forward, I started educating myself on Good Clinical Practice (GCP) and 21 CFR (Code 0f Federal Regulations Title 21), the major regulations and guidance we needed to adhere to as a company.

Frank was very well versed on these topics, but he kept it to himself unless you asked him a question. Then after a meandering soliloquy you might get your answer – usually a yes or no that could have been delivered in 10 seconds.

Over the course of the first three months, we made some progress working through Frank, but I could see we could move 100 times faster with him out of the way. After three months I felt that I knew enough to tell Boris we could dispense with Frank and find ourselves more of a team player to lead QA. Boris agreed, but before we could execute, the division president chimed in with "concerns." She was Frank's friend and they both spent way too much time conspiring against the chairman and dreaming of when they would rule the earth. Boris ignored her advice and took mine.

Admittedly it took us longer to find the right person for QA. We went through a few different people before getting one to stick. But during that time, we totally re-did our process – what's termed our quality management system (QMS). Further, as we were subject to external audits regularly, I am proud to announce that our re-written QMS always received high marks, including one auditor that termed it "first rate." High praise from an auditor.

The gloom and doom predicted by the division president never arrived and we never failed an audit or lost a bid due to failures or flaws in our QMS. My gut had told me we didn't need the "oracle" and that I was capable for filling the gap as needed. After all, all these regulations are written down, well organized and fairly brief. You just have to know how to read.

When I took over talent acquisition at Clinical, I was floored when I saw just how much time and energy we were putting into getting candidates drug tested. I was shocked by how long it took, and how many times we weren't able to confirm an offer in a timely manner because we were waiting for the test. Further, the few times in the past when we got a positive result, we had overruled our own policy and hired the candidate anyway. "This is crazy," I told the chairman and head of finance, also somewhat libertarian in their thinking. "We need to stop this unnecessary expense and crazy waste of time." They agreed and drug testing at Clinical ended. The world did not end, no sponsors ever asked what our drug testing policy was, and no bongs suddenly appeared on the conference room tables.

One last story, which involves listening as well as trusting one's gut. It also explores a third area, taking care of your own best interest. I include it here because trusting yourself (and your gut) to do something with what you heard really matters. In late 2017 / early 2018, Clinical got an unsolicited offer from an India-based CRO looking to establish a US presence. They did their due diligence and made us a proposal that was in round numbers about $.45/share if we met certain stretch revenue and profit objectives for the rest of 2018. If we didn't meet those goals the price would fall to around $.25/share.

Aside from the fact I didn't see much of a future in this path for me (I'm sure they had their own compliance and IT executives), it seemed like they were setting us up to fail and then get the company for next to nothing.

We had always marketed and prided ourselves that we weren't just another CRO. We claimed our competitors were slow, lacked proper project management, were disjointed with their work-from-home models, and prone to failure. At one point, our motto was "many rescues, never rescued," meaning we had taken over failing projects from other CROs but had never had one taken away from us.

Going with the India-based CRO would mean tossing that whole positioning strategy out the door and then rebuilding our internal culture, which employees had come to accept as a matter of faith, that we were better.

To evaluate the offer and make a decision, we had a conference call with our business broker, Shane, whom we had hired to assist us. (As a side note, Shane had been following us and talking with Boris for some time – he has the skills of listening and asking for what he wants.) Sitting in the room on the call with me were Boris, his wife Larisa (our head of finance), and the head of operations. Essentially Boris and Larisa owned the vast majority of the stock with the head of operations being the largest holder after them. I was by far the smallest shareholder and essentially the only outsider. The other three were all one family (the head of operations was for all intents and purposes

Boris and Larisa's daughter, having grown up with the company for over 10 years right out of college).

As Shane talked, he mentioned an alternative strategy, private equity. According to him, under a private equity deal we would maintain some part of the business and then participate a second time in a sale when the equity partner sought to cash in their investment. My ears perked up when he said that, but I could see that Boris's mind was somewhere else and Larisa and operations were both just wanting to grab the cash offered from India and be done with it all.

I stopped the call, interrupting Shane and repeated back to him what he had just said, asking for confirmation. He confirmed. That got Boris's attention, asking if he had heard and understood what Shane had just said. He came back to the moment and we proceeded to discuss.

I knew Boris would like the idea of a chance for more money and keeping control. He liked being chairman. I can't blame him, as I also wanted more money and keeping control, and I liked my job, too. Larisa and the head of operations expressed concerns, both of them wanting to just be done and rest as much as anything. But even they could see this was a chance at a much better deal, and, like it or not, Boris was jumping on board.

Shane then officially put us on the market and took us through a variety of meetings with interested parties. Eventually we partnered with a private equity firm in a deal structured just the way Shane said it would be.

Things may not have worked out exactly as planned. Still, by my math, regardless of what happens now, we're still ahead of where we would have been in the best-case scenario under the first offer.

Now, had I not been listening, it would have been easy to miss Shane's comments on private equity. Then, if I didn't trust myself, have confidence in my understanding and interpretation of the meaning of the private equity concept and just kept my mouth shut, we would have likely just sold out to India and been done. That would have grossly undervalued the business and left all of us unemployed much sooner.

We talked about making decisions when all the analysis is inconclusive and no clear winner emerges. Make no mistake, these decisions are tough. But with experience, you'll get better at making them. You have no choice. You can't say, "Oh, this is a tough one. I'll pass." You can't sit down at the table and after the cards are dealt, say "Never mind." No, you either decide or get comfortable not having to decide, since nobody will be asking. And, that's not good.

Making good decisions is what separates leaders, effective executives, and successful people from everyone else. Good decisions are measured not just by outcomes but by how much time and money was spent to make them. If you need a full analysis of restaurant options in the city before deciding where to have dinner, watch out. You may want to look at something less taxing than business management. If you're a fast decider but every decision turns into a disaster, go sit with the dinner planner. No, you need to combine good, logical analytics with a bias for action (move) and trust in your gut to get there fast.

In conclusion:
    a. You're your own best friend.
    b. Trust yourself (your gut), because it's your experience talking.
    c. There is risk of a bad decision, but once the hand is dealt, you have to play it.

Conversation 10 – Communicate

While good listening skills are critical, there's going to come a time in your career when you'll have to start to provide outbound communication. As you move from someone doing the work to someone directing others to do it and eventually to deciding what it is you're going to do, you'll need to start talking. And once you start, you need to keep doing it, again and again and again.

There's a maxim that the US military used to use for presentations: "Tell them what you're going to tell them, tell them, tell them what you told them." That's pretty good advice for not just presentations but communicating in general. If you want your team to do x and you'd like x to get done efficiently and effectively, you can't just say "do x." You've got to tell them multiple times and in multiple forums. Then you need to check in and tell them again.

As you move into not only directing your staff but explaining new ideas or programs to others in the company, your messaging will need to be consistently repeated multiple times and through multiple channels, such as presentations, emails, one-on-one conversations, small groups, and status updates.

Depending on the scope of what you're doing and who is impacted, communication can become a full-time job. The president of the United States has an entire office dedicated to just communication. Okay, you might not be the US president, but in some positions the communication requirements are still more than a single person can handle. If it's your message that needs communicating, you'll need to set up a process that not only gets the message out to all the required constituencies, but also gets the same message out, has a feedback loop to ensure it's working, and a rapid response capability to listen for and correct any misinformation before it takes hold.

In the business world, no matter how much (and how well) you communicate, the message will get corrupted somewhere along the way and you'll need to correct that. In addition, once you start communicating, you have to continue. If you're not putting messages out there, they will create themselves.

How is that even possible?

Lots of ways. Members of your team who are trying to be helpful might be communicating messages. Folks who are opposed to your project may be doing a little sabotage. It might just be that previously communicated information that has become distorted over time as it is continually repeated. Wherever the bogus communication is coming from, the only way to fight it is to keep the official communication channel continuously refreshed, full and moving.

Now, up to this point I've been speaking as if we're dealing with internal projects. However, the exact same principle applies to external communication. That might be communication on products and services, or on new and exciting offers or updates. Whether it's internal or external, what's required is continuous, consistent, and complete communication.

How should I write my communications? Should I send presentations in advance? Are phone calls better than emails?

Wow, hold on. I was hesitant to put this conversation in this book because it is so large on its own. But, it's also the elephant in the room that we can't just ignore. Rather than try to go into great detail here, let me give you a few pointers to get you by and then we'll have to see about creating another book just for Communication.

Here are Uncle Gary's Quick Rules of Communication:

1) Communication needs to be Continuous, Consistent, Complete and Concise.
2) Remember the audience and communicate to that level, and remember that all communications you write won't be the same. A communication on the new lunchroom schedule needs to be written differently than one explaining the financial impact of a new acquisition. Formality, word choice, structure, medium, and similar factors will vary.
3) Base the choice of communication medium on target audience and message complexity and importance. If you're communicating the new lunchroom schedule to employees, an email and some posters or notices in the lunchroom would be appropriate. If you're communicating the sale of the company, an all-hands meeting and presentation with

Q&A would be the better route. It's the same audience in both cases, just the importance and complexity of what's being communicated is different.
4) Remember KIS – Keep It Simple. Regardless of the material being communicated, strive to keep it simple. Your goal in communicating is to get others to understand. Highly complex material may require "big words" and technical jargon, but the structure of the communication doesn't have to automatically get more complicated. A series of bullet points in an email may turn out to be more effective than long narrative paragraphs or a large PowerPoint deck.
5) Plan for communication; it shouldn't be just an afterthought. Good communication doesn't just happen by itself. It needs to be planned (who, what, when, how, why), written and edited, produced, delivered, and reinforced. This just won't happen, so allow time and resources to get it done.

I hope this gives you some insight into the importance of communication and how to do it yourself. As I said, this topic is worthy of a book on its own. Many exist and I would recommend you pick one up to get a more detailed grounding in this critical topic. For now, keep the points presented here in mind.

Illustrative Cases:

Can you share an example of a strategy document?

No. A corporate communication strategy for a business or for a major internal initiative can run to book size on its own. Instead I'll give a little story from Clinical. The summer after I joined the company, Miami was threatened by a potential hurricane. Boris was in Europe and his wife Larisa (the head of finance) was in California visiting family. At that time we had no official policy nor any official chain of command except Boris – then probably Larisa, then everyone else. Absent the first two, the "everyone else" started moving. Each department started doing its own things. Anyone who attended the regular management meeting began issuing contradictory orders, most of which seemed to center around when to leave and what to do with the plastic bags that suddenly seemed to be everywhere. Frankly, with all the confusion and running around, I considered just putting one of those bags over my head.

Rather than add my voice the cacophony, I chose to make a note to write a business continuity plan with clear instruction on the chain of command and how to communicate next time. I also monitored the storm, determining that it was likely to turn away but would pass close enough to our beachside offices to warrant protecting assets and preparing our staff to work from home.

The storm passed and I wrote the business continuity plan. It was short, because without knowing the precise nature of the future disaster we might face, how much can you say? But, the plan was clear. To start with, the chain of command was Boris and then me. I reasoned that I was most likely to be in the office and I had done extensive disaster planning work both at Ryder and with one of my consulting clients. The second key component of the plan was that we would plan a communication tree, where messages would go out from the disaster leader through email, and each manager would be responsible for confirming that each of their direct reports had gotten the message and as appropriate had confirmed that *their* directs had done so, all the way down through the organization.

    I got Boris's signature on the plan to make it all official and then filed it away until needed or auditors asked to see it.

    A few years later, we faced Hurricane Irma and we had to put the plan into effect. Boris was technically in town, but he was one of the first ones at the airport, so the responsibility for managing the process fell to me. I was fully expecting this. So, three times daily I issued an email communication. At first, these messages tracked the storm and issued instructions on how to prepare. Later, after we had evacuated the office, the emails continued to report on the storm's status, reminders to employees to focus first on their own and their family's safety, and then on work activities (if feasible). After the storm had passed, the emails provided updates on the office's reopening until we were back in and officially closed out the disaster. I got a lot of positive feedback on those emails.

    Why?

    For a few reasons. First, as a company we did not have a good track record of communicating anything. This time we had communicated and done so not once but consistently throughout the several days it took for the storm to pass and the office to reopen. Second, the communications were clear and concise. I didn't write long paragraphs, just a structured list of bullet points. Further, it was easy to track if you'd missed anything because I numbered each communication. If you were suddenly reading number 15 but the prior one you saw was 13, you would know you missed 14 and could seek it out. And lastly, I was inclusive. Everyone, even employees outside of Florida, got the same email. In that way, other offices would know what was going on and would not be in the dark.

As it turned out, we shut the office for about four days. Staff and management were spread all over the US, from Los Angeles to Chicago. No projects stopped, no projects reported any significant issues. We worked effectively and resumed normal operations without a glitch.

This little story points out what is important about communication. It was continuous, consistent and complete. And in this case, since we were communicating to large audiences, it needed to be concise. The emails were bulleted, not narrative in nature, clearly dated and time stamped, and limited in scope to items of immediate import, not speculation on the what-ifs.

In conclusion:
a. Remember the 4 Cs – Continuous, Consistent, Complete, Concise.
b. Remember the audience and communicate to the appropriate level.

c. Base your choice of communication medium on target audience, message importance, and message complexity.
d. Remember KIS – Keep It Simple.
e. Plan for communication.

Conversation 11 - Lead

They say leaders are born not made. I don't agree with that. But, I do believe they are made very early in life, and in business. All business leaders share some key traits. They're trustworthy, consistent, loyal, respectful of others, and passionate in their beliefs. In addition to these traits, they of course demonstrate the other skills highlighted in this book. These aren't hereditary traits or skills; they're learned. But, some of them you could learn by kindergarten and use the rest of your life.

As discussed in the previous conversation, communication is essential to success in business. And it is a vital skill for leaders to possess. This would include written and verbal communication. You need to be able to express yourself so that others understand what you are leading them to do.

You don't have to be a great orator, you just need to be clear, consistent and truthful in what you say and write. You also don't have to be a super high-energy cheerleader. You need energy to be successful in business, but directed energy. If it's not your style to be jumping up on the conference table and leading the team in a rousing cheer, don't worry. That works for some people, but only when it's consistent with who they are. If you're more reserved, that's okay too. Just be yourself, but communicate.

Throughout my career, there were many times when everyone in the room was lower grades or the same grade and there was no named leader, or the person who supposedly was the boss froze. Unfortunately, this often occurred during a crisis. It's in those moments that I believe true leaders emerge. Anyone can lead when draped in the trappings of high office surrounded with an army of staff who officially report to you. True leadership is seizing the reins when the horses are stampeding and everyone in the wagon looks sick.

If you want to be a leader, act like one and lead. Don't sit around complaining about how things are, propose new processes or other changes to make them better and then be sure to carry them out if accepted.

Take charge in a crisis. Just do it. Don't wait for permission; when everyone is looking for somebody to step up, be that person. Call out things that are wrong when you see them happening and set people straight. If you see abusive behavior being perpetrated by a manager, call them on it, even if they don't work for you and even if they're your peer.

Be passionate about the business but realistic. Cheerleading is not leadership. Leaders are on the field, not on the sidelines.

If you just lead, you'll be amazed how quickly people will follow. And, the next time something comes along, how naturally they'll turn to you as the leader. Leadership has its privileges, but it is truly a position of responsibility. You are not only responsible for the work products produced, but also responsible for your team. You need to be concerned with their growth and learning just as much as the completion of tasks.

Taking on the leadership mantle means you are taking on that extra responsibility, which in the long run can be the most personally rewarding.

One of the greatest pleasures is when former colleagues thank me or tell others that they learned from me and attribute part of their success to me. I have a number of associates who went on to be captains of industry, highly successful entrepreneurs, and even chairmen of public company boards. I've even had people I had to dismiss see me later and thank me for giving them a push in the right direction.

I'm proud of all of them, and hope that in some small way they did learn something from me.

If you familiarize yourself with the points in this book, you'll be up to the challenge of leadership and obtaining your own success while also leading future generations in ways that will allow them to achieve theirs.

Illustrative Cases:

One story of this came my way shortly after I joined the contract research organization (CRO). I was having a hallway conversation (remember those things?) with the vice president (VP) of operations, who casually mentioned something about sending some staff in Eastern Europe to clean up some issues at some sites from an old study. As it turns out, the study in question was before the US Food and Drug Administration (FDA) as part of the standard process for approval of new drug therapies. Based on its review of the study data and supporting documentation, the FDA had asked for an audit. Having been given this heads-up by the client, the head of operations was trying to get ahead of the curve and fix things before the audit. And as this was a 100% audit of every data point and document, it would be impossible to do in the time allowed.

Fast-forward a few months and we were presented with an audit of the study sites in Eastern Europe. It was not pretty. In fact, the auditor had gone out of their way to throw mud at us. In quite a few cases the mud was totally unjustified or grossly exaggerated. However, there still was enough meat in the report to require a complete response.

This audit report was series business and required serious work, but the first thing we had to do was maintain an appearance of calm and cooperation in front of the client as we looked at the volume of findings. Seeing that Boris was too prone to ranting and not thinking clearly and the VP of operations was too far down in the weeds, I took charge of orchestrating our response. First, I got us to categorize the detailed issues into related groups, and then created a section-by-section rebuttal of what issues we could, clarification on those that we found to be wrong, and corrections for any remaining. All this was presented in a structured report that was easy to read and follow, coupled with multiple meetings and phone calls with the client where we demonstrated cooperation and professionalism throughout.

I was aided in the heavy lifting portions by John, head of data sciences, and Mark, the head of safety, both experts in critical areas of clinical trials. They were supported by the VP of operations and her team in collating the findings and tracking down source documents.

In the end, a disaster was averted. Relations with the client remained professional and no blood was spilt.

Now, why did others; my peers, even the chairman, let me take control? Cynics might say because they didn't want this thing in their lap. But, I believe it's because they saw something in me and were comfortable standing back a little.

From my days in school and earliest career days, I found people had a tendency to listen to me, follow my direction, and look to me for guidance. Now I'm not stupid but I'm also not Einstein, nor am I a matinee idol. Yet, people gravitated to me. That was in spite of, as mentioned earlier in this book, the fact that during the first years of my career I was a bit of an introvert, even going so far as attending the Dale Carnegie course to break some of those habits. So what is it?

My belief is that people just see those traits I mentioned in me. I'm trusting, I don't lie, and I'm worthy of trust because I do my homework and am knowledgeable on the things I speak about.

I'm loyal and respectful. I never toss my teams under the bus and will stand in front of the bus myself rather than see them get run over. If there's going to be any discipline, coaching and management of my team, I'll do it. If they failed at some task, it's because I didn't prepare them or manage them well enough.

I'm consistent, I don't take one position today, another tomorrow and a third after the weekend. I will change based on facts and good arguments, but I don't flip-flop around trying to guess which way the wind is blowing. I've never said, "I was for it before I was against it," as so many politicians seem to do.

Lastly, I'm passionate about the things I believe in and I obviously believe I've got the skills in this book, because I wrote the book.

Now if you're blessed to have obtained the right set of traits and enough of the skills to function, leadership opportunities will gravitate to you. Sometimes that will come in terms of official titles, other times it will just be the de facto operating model.

During the implementation of the SSC at Ryder, there were two of us at the front of the project. I was a group manager from IT officially tasked with making the IT changes necessary to accomplish the goal. A group director from finance (the person who later asked if I had shit for brains) was the overall project head and eventual head of the SSC. However, there was no doubt who people looked to for answers, guidance and help no matter what the topic. While respect was paid to the organization chart, I just did what was necessary and the team followed – business and IT alike.

However, I had no official staff reporting to me. You could look on any organization chart and find I was a box unto myself. Then why did senior managers and directors in finance follow me? How did I get the various subgroups within IT to do what needed to be done? Leadership.

I talked to these people and practiced my listening to hear what was on their mind, instead of just talking and dropping demands on them. I sought first to understand. I expressed empathy with their situation, workload, and issues, but then transitioned back to what I needed and how it could help them in their job.

When problems arose and tempers were flaring, I kept the folks working on my behalf out of the line of fire, I took the shots and left them to just do what they did best. A good story is the decision to go with Dell desktops at the SSC instead of the then-company-standard Compaq.

What's a Compact?

C O M P A Q, Compaq. They were a computer hardware company, actually a leader for a number of years. Some of the earliest portable computers were Compaqs. They were merged with Hewlett-Packard several years ago and the brand has disappeared. But at that time and place, this was a major flash point escalating all the way to the senior vice president (SVP) controller.

He was concerned with reliability and Dells were new to the market. The secret to their success was that they were assembling parts from a variety of OEMs to make a Dell computer. Thus two Dells with the same model number might not share exactly the same parts inside.

The chief information officer (CIO) had issued the edict that he wanted a second brand so that we weren't reliant on one supplier and could maintain some negotiating leverage. The SSC offered the perfect place to make a substantial step toward achieving that goal. On the other hand, due to their internal differences, there was some possibility that one Dell box might not perform the same as another Dell box.

Personally, I would have preferred the Compaqs just because I felt I was being pushed out on the tip of the spear while the CIO remained comfortably in his office. On the other hand, with some good testing, we could largely eliminate the danger of any surprises down the road.

After some screaming, spitting, and blue language directed at me, the SVP gave up and we put in the Dells.

The SSC opened as planned, and I think it was truly one of IT's finest hours because they came together as a team to make it all happen. I was recognized for my role and even though I didn't have any staff was considered by all to have led the efforts.

One year after joining Ryder I had been promoted to director and was in charge of the financial applications for the corporation, billing/invoicing systems for leasing, and the SSC support. At this time the corporate CIO essentially threw up his hands and convinced management to outsource IT. A year-long process was undertaken which eventually resulted in the alliance with Accenture and IBM. At the time the alliance was coming into existence, I assumed I'd either be going back to work for Accenture as they absorbed the Ryder application development teams, or be laid off.

I was surprised one morning when the CFO for the leasing division came into my office and asked if I was anxious to go back to Accenture or if I would consider staying with Ryder. I had met Tracy a few times and knew who she was, but we had never worked together on anything. Yet there she was offering me a promotion and, more importantly, the chance to lead a $100 million part of Ryder. I said yes.

Why did she pick me? I can't say for sure, but I most definitely believe the leadership traits I noted above played a role.

As the alliance moved forward, I'll admit there were some tough days. Days I didn't live up to my own standards. Days I could have used this book to help guide me. But from some of those dark days, I learned lessons that helped me to more firmly believe in and hold on to these teachings.

While I had been picked to stay with Ryder, the contracting was still going on. A key milestone in the negotiations was that Accenture would deliver a procedures manual before the contract would be signed. As the head of Ryder IT (at least the leasing division and corporate systems), I was designated to receive and review the procedure manual when it came in order to give the OK.

One day I was in the hall and the CIO, Bruce, who was leading the negotiations for Ryder before he left the company, came up to me and asked if I had received the procedures manual. I said, "No, they gave me an index to a procedure manual but not the manual itself." He thanked me and then went back into a conference room.

Within a matter of minutes I was beset by Accenture partners, managers and staff, all babbling excitedly. "What did you say, what did you say?" they clamored.

"About what?" I asked.

"What did you tell Bruce?"

Oh, now I understood. So I told them what I'd said to Bruce. "I got an index to a procedures manual but not the procedures manual itself." That's what I had been given, what else did they expect me to say? To this day I wonder if they expected me to exaggerate in their favor because of old times.

The Accenture horde looked very dejected and disgusted, but went back into the conference room. I don't know what was said in there afterwards, but the result was that Ryder signed without the procedures manual, but with a promise that one would be coming. It came indeed; my team and I wrote it. We had a nice young staffer from Accenture do the typing, but we crafted the content and wrote it. I should have sent them an invoice.

What's sad is that the hallway circus was just the beginning of a relationship that went downhill from there. To be clear, I had no axe to grind. I was thinking of all the great things I'd be able to accomplish with Accenture and IBM to do the heavy lifting for me. But it wasn't meant to be. To be fair, IBM did their part well. They just moved at IBM speed, which, back then at least, you measured in tree rings.

Accenture, well, that was a battle that escalated into full-scale war. Various partners would be brought in, listen to my concerns and specific issues. Each time they'd nod their heads in agreement, then leave my office to meet with the partner assigned to our account, never to be seen or heard from again.

Three years on, there was no solution but divorce. One of my last tasks at Ryder was to negotiate the divorce agreement. Technically they were revisions to the alliance agreement, but everyone knew they were just the way to open the door to a bloodless separation. Everyone was exhausted by then.

In conclusion:
  a. If you lead, others will follow.
  b. Leaders often emerge in a crisis.
  c. Communication is key to effective leadership.
  d. Leadership has privileges but also major responsibilities; you need to accept both.
  e. Leadership can be the most rewarding part of a business career due to its impact on others.

Conversation 12 – Form Alliances

Almost everything you want to accomplish in business that's of any significance will involve more than one part of the business. You might not need some other team to help do the work, but what you do may impact them in some way. Or, you may need their buy-in to get funding, or it might be a collegial culture where the expectation is that big ideas are signed off on by the group.

Any way you slice it, rarely will you be able to make big change happen alone.

To accomplish these activities then, you're going to need to form alliances. In my book, alliances are defined as temporary associations put together to accomplish a common objective. They're not friendships, although you could also have an alliance with a friend. No they are purely commercial and transactional in nature.

By this I mean they are formed for a specific purpose – implement the new xxx system – and their duration is only for as long as required to complete that purpose. Alliances will come and go, new alliances for new needs will form, often with similar members as before but not necessarily. You'll need specific expertise, depending on the nature of what it is you want to achieve. .

Where this leads you to is that you'll need to maintain at least open business communication and working relationships with all the key players in the company. You can't afford to be in open warfare with anyone because you don't know when you may need their help or their participation in an alliance. You need to be Switzerland.

How do you do that?

First, practice and become expert at that fine art of listening. If you're listening and not talking while others are bitching and complaining, you can avoid stepping into a trap and unnecessarily choosing sides on some issue that is not your concern.

You listen, you're empathetic, but you don't commit. Stay on good terms with both parties in any internal dispute, even if you think one may be right. If it's not your fight and you get nothing from the ultimate answer, why jump in? Even if the side you pick wins, you've just made an enemy of the other side and they will be more upset with you than the original party to the conflict.

Why?

The original party had a reason for being engaged, while you were just an opinionated outsider who decided to jump in.

To be able to build an effective alliance, you will need to maintain a working rapport with others. You can't afford to make enemies. While you can and should disagree professionally when appropriate, you don't need to go out of you way to become involved in things that don't really matter, or become belligerent in any disagreement you do need to have.

Keep your cards close to your vest, let no one know everything you're thinking or all the cards you're holding. You don't need to be ruthless, but you do need to be smart and cautious.

This sounds like office politics?

Well, it's more like diplomacy. When I think of office politics I think more of one hand washes the other, where you're in it for personal gain, not to accomplish something for the company. My diplomacy analogy comes from the need to maintain open communication at all times with the ability to form some sort of mutual aid agreement as needed.

At the end of the day, you'll find that there will be many times that you need someone else's help to complete your projects or your work. To obtain that help, you will have to form transitory relationships with other groups that will come and go, depending on the projects in play at any point in time.

Illustrative Cases:

Let me tell a story to illustrate. While at Ryder, before the Accenture/IBM alliance came in, there had been a team working on developing a new custom vehicle maintenance solution. After the Accenture/IBM alliance, that team became part of Accenture. Very quickly, Accenture began to cast doubts on the effort and within a couple months came forward and said that it just technically couldn't be done. I believed them to be right.

A meeting with the head of maintenance and his key direct report confirmed that they also weren't full sold on the strategy -- not for technical reasons but for business process reasons. The effort had started under a previous administration and was sort of an insider's game between the then-head of maintenance and the IT project director at that time. With nobody stepping up to own the project, and the consultant saying that the as-is design would not work, there no choice but to pull the plug.

So what next? At this time the big debate was around integration. How much should you try to put into an integrated enterprise system versus running a set of "best of breed" point solutions for each area and then trying to tie things together on the back side? Personally I was in favor of the integrated solution. Heavy lifting maybe to get there, but once achieved, simplicity and expandability would be the order of the day.

While the maintenance team was open to the idea, they were still very narrowly focused on their specific needs. But, I did have a possible ally in the head of purchasing.

The head of purchasing handled basic purchasing (office supplies, etc.), vehicle parts, and vehicles. She also was the president of the small side business we had that sold parts. Most of the sales were internal, but she and I were working on a website to allow for external sales, pretty visionary at the time. In addition to that, we were also putting in SAP to support the parts business operations as part of the company's overall Y2K efforts.

We were both proponents of the SAP model and saw the wisdom of an integrated solution that would give us full visibility of the vehicle from order to onboarding it to putting it into service. She and I formed an alliance. She wasn't my friend, and there were other efforts where we were on opposite sides of an issue, but for this effort, we were bound together.

We then began the process of converting the maintenance head and his director into true believers, which we did. Collectively then, that three-party alliance was able to take on the herculean task of getting a $50 million initiative approved, which we did.

It was a lot of work, lot of give and take, particularly around the outside consultants we hired. I had to give on that one when my horse (KPMG) somehow managed to step on itself. Ultimately, the effort withered, as mentioned in the introduction to this book; organizational change drove the three alliance members out of the company and there was no one left inside to lead the effort. It staggered on, but a change of that magnitude needed the full alliance to be successful. Instead, it was an orphan.

Another story of an alliance in action was with TALOS at Clinical. Here, I could not get the project management team to take any interest even though the purpose of the system was to be the program management engine. However, the clinical management team – the team that did the real hands-on work of site visit reviews (which is what much of the work is about) – was interested. Therefore, to keep momentum, we worked on building out parts of the system that supported their activities. These were necessary, but they were sort of standalone application modules and were really the same type of functionality that one would find in a Clinical Trail Management System CTMS.

Some of the high flyers that passed overhead would point that out to me. "And?" I would ask. We needed that functionality, and by building it custom we were simply laying the foundation stones for the ultimate solution of linking everything with the automation of the business processes. And, since the Clinical team wanted to collaborate, why not go that route rather than keep trying to drag along the uninterested?

The ultimate goal was to eventually tie them together with the process-driven management part of the system where, instead of going to a screen and entering data, the user would sign in and be presented with a list of the day's tasks. When they clicked a task it would give them whatever they needed to complete it, including a screen for data input if that was required.

The point was that I needed this functionality and whether I did it at that moment or a year from that point was not relevant. It was something where I had an eager user to work with, and we elected to move forward while others waited.

In conclusion:
a. Maintain a constructive rapport with everyone.
b. Construct and deconstruct alliance relationships as required by current activities.
c. Use outside providers as needed.

Conversation 13 – It's In the Contract

As with everything in this book, I'm speaking here based on my own experience. I am not a lawyer, but I've written, reviewed, rewritten and negotiated innumerable contracts and similar agreements. The most two important components of a good contract are:

1) Keeping it simple, and
2) Putting it away and never looking at it after signing.

The more complicated you allow a contract to get, the more likely you're setting yourself up for failure. Hidden in all that complexity will be little land mines that will go off when you least expect them. You may think you're really putting the screws to the other party but in the end you'll only be putting the screws to yourself.

I'm not sure I understand what a land mine is. Is it a penalty?

It could be; that would be one type of landmine. Others may be more subtle. For example, a clause that says if a certain number of penalties occur in a specific time frame, some other much more serious clause kicks in. Often in contracts where the lawyers were left alone to do the writing, you'll end up with something approaching mutually assured destruction. Effectively, you'll get a contract that neither side can fully satisfy and therefore each side is entitled to extraordinary relief. Bottom line: a contract that strayed far from its purpose. That's why business people, not attorneys, need to have the ultimate say on these matters. And trust me, if your legal team starts to bitch, ask them who's signing the contract at the end. It won't be them. With a big deal, your ass is on the line. Absolutely listen to whatever good legal advice you can get. But don't let lawyers pull you into the dark paranoia that is too often their world.

After all, why are you entering into this arrangement in the first place? Presumably it's because you and someone else each have something the other wants or needs to achieve their goals. You may have money and the other party may have goods or services you need. Or both of you may have goods or services which when combined together can form some greater benefit. Whatever the reason is, it's likely not to go screw the other guy.

For all contracts, the best advice is let the lawyers handle the indemnity clause and other standard legal terms. But, you should take a business law class and then personally handle the business terms. Try to negotiate win/win terms and be very cautious of any penalties and deadlines, as those can come back to bite you regardless of which side of the deal you're on. Lastly, read the thing cover to cover at least once before you sign.

Remember, you want to work with this other party; the goal isn't to be punitive and penalize them. If you don't think they're going to perform, don't pick them. Remember the Golden Rule, "Do unto others as you would have them do unto you."

Illustrative Cases:

To illustrate, I go back to the alliance at Ryder with Accenture and IBM. This contract was anything but simple. It was a 4-inch thick binder of double-sided pages detailing every aspect of how this arrangement to manage Ryder's IT would be conducted. And, buried in it were an uncountable number of little land mines that did nothing but get in the way and cause pain. To be clear, I wasn't yet in charge when the contract was written. I was asked to meet on one or two sections, but never saw the whole document until it was signed. In fact, I don't think anybody at Ryder really read the whole thing. We relied too much on our consultants to help us. And when you step back and think about it, while they were going to be dealing with us once, they worked closely with Accenture and IBM on a regular basis. In retrospect, maybe we weren't the big dogs we thought we were and we really should have stayed on the porch and let the big ones hunt.

Back to the Ryder alliance contract. Further complicating matters, while my division was effectively the sole user of the services (the other division having wiggled out of it), Corporate Ryder took on the task of administering the contract. And, they chose a new lawyer to lead that task.

Charts were made and soon all discussion was around each date and each metric in the contract.

One of the little land mine was a clause that the alliance had to take on a certain percentage of the former Ryder employees. If the percentage wasn't met, the alliance would have to pay a penalty to Ryder. This clause was slipped in by Ryder, because it was trying to limit severance costs. It did that, but it also resulted in us having to keep the same people working on our account, just at about twice the cost. Brilliant.

Another little beauty was this elaborate set of charts that showed service levels for numerous things. Each chart showed a band, with the lower limit of the band representing the point where if the Alliance fell below it, they would again face a penalty in terms of money owed back to Ryder. The upper band was the aspirational goal.

For some reason, the very bright finance people and business people at Ryder (and I am very serious when I say bright people, as at that time there were some serious financial brains working there) thought that meant the alliance would be looking to improve service. Why? There was no incentive for doing better, just a penalty for failure to meet some minimum standard which they of course had negotiated down to a very low base level.

I still recall the meeting when this fact finally became clear. We were having one of our very senior-level meetings and I asked the question directly to both the Accenture partner and IBM vice president in attendance. Were they working to achieve the stretch, aspirational service levels listed? The IBM VP's answer was succinct: "No." He then went on to explain what anybody should have known. They would work very hard to stay above the minimum service line since they did not want to pay any penalties, but they had no interest or intention to strive for anything better since there was nothing in it for them.

The Accenture partner's answer was silence. No reply. Obviously it was the same goal, he just lacked the balls to say it. We thanked IBM for their candor, and said we now understood the rules better and would work within that set of facts.

In my consulting business, UPi, I have managed to keep it simple when it comes to contracting with clients. I still rely on an arrangement letter format, which is what we used to do at the Firm when I first joined. The letter outlines the scope of work, estimates fees and expenses, any rates agreed to, and an expected timeline. Since our work is usually very open ended and dependent on client availability, participation and decision-making, I've always refused to lock myself into anything more. I'm lucky and understand some situations call for tighter, more formal, contracts.

While I was with Capgemini, we had to have contracts for our outsourced services deals. Having learned from the alliance situation, I fought to keep those simple. We had defined service levels but we didn't let penalties in. Our argument was that if we weren't providing the services, they had the ultimate penalty to use against us, cancel the contract. But, if they had individual monthly penalties for missing some metric, all we would do would be to focus on those metrics and nothing else. Most clients bought the concept.

But they had the ability to cancel the whole contract if you didn't perform?

Well, they always have that right, even with the penalty clauses. And, here's a little secret, changing providers for the types of services we were offering was not a trivial exercise. Most clients took more than a year to make the decision to hire someone, then find them, and then get them on board. Few want to do it again.

In conclusion:
 a. Avoid complexity and confusion of words.
 b. Think win/win.
 c. Put the contract away once it's signed.

Conversation 14 – Expect Change

As I first started to write this Conversation, I had it as number 4. As I began to write, I realized it belonged last. You need all the skills and ideas discussed in all the other Conversations to succeed in handling Change. So, since it's my book, I moved it.

There are probably as many books, seminars and consulting hours spent on change management as there are on goals. Well, you're in luck, I'm not talking about change management here. I'm talking about expecting change – thus the Conversation title. No matter what endeavor you've embarked on, how well the business is doing, how happy everyone is working together and how beautiful and sunny the day is, circumstances will change.

Now this could be positive change: business gets even better, more sales, more happy customers, even more great coworkers and a super-great new boss. Or, it could be negative change with all that means. It really doesn't matter; positive or negative, the status quo will not last. Hell, that's a fundamental law of physics. The Universe is always trying to move from order to disorder. Business is not exempt.

The stories that follow all turned out to have some negative outcome associated with the change, even if the change itself was a good thing. As I wrote this and wracked my brain for a meaningful positive story, I was stymied but not surprised. For those of you who are currently in business, you know this; for those about to join, you'll soon learn it. If you have any type of management role you are damn busy every day, fighting things right in front of you. You have precious little time to ponder and think through the what-ifs. I'm not trying to make excuses, just stating a fact. But, as the following stoires show, it might be wise to carve out some time to ponder what could change and how you would address it. It might save a lot of heartache later on. Switching gears just a little before I give some examples of Change, no conversation on Change would be complete without some discussion about the biggest change of all, changing jobs. This activity, in a word, I hate.

That may sound strange, given my consulting background. But changing clients is not nearly the same as changing jobs. Changing clients means getting an opportunity to learn new things, go new places, meet new people, and solve new issues. While changing jobs offers those same benefits, it also means changing one's self. You need to adopt to the new culture, change loyalties if you go with a competitor, establish new alliances, establish new mentor/mentee relationships, and navigate a minefield of potential issues. And, surprisingly, rarely do clients conduct personal interviews of people assigned to their projects. You will meet them in the proposal process and undoubtedly they're sizing you up, but it's not that formal interview process you find in job hunting. Like, where do you see yourself in 10 years? I'm 62 -- hopefully still looking at the green side of the grass.

However, there are occasions when changing jobs cannot or should not be avoided. Obviously if you lose your job, you'll need to find another. Or, if your job isn't going to offer you the opportunity to get where you want to go, you either need to change your ambitions or move on to something else. There is a third reason, and this is to try and job-hop your way to the top.

I've seen several of these folks over my career. They're sort of like bees, flitting from flower to flower but never staying long in one place. They're usually very charming and talk a good game, but it's hard to say what they ever really did, since they never seem to stick around long enough to reap the benefits or consequences of any actions they may take.

I've seen successful bees, but I've also seen several that have a little success and then hit a wall and fall. If you want to be a bee, you'd probably better go find another book on that. I can't provide much help.

However, there is one piece of advice I can offer to all job seekers, and for this I have to thank a former boss and all-around good guy, Don Tomlin, "Always run to something, never away".

Illustrative Cases:

The first story of change that wasn't planned for and thus resulted in a crash was the implementation of SAP to support the procurement and fleet maintenance functions at Ryder. This was a large project that required the coordination and support of procurement, operations, fleet maintenance and IT to come together on a shared vision, select a path to achieve that vision and then obtain buy-in and funding from the most senior levels in the company.

We achieved that and began the actual design and implementation work.

What we had not counted on nor planned for was our own demise. Shortly after the project was kicked off, the company had a new CEO and the VP procurement, SVP operations, VP maintenance and VP IT (me) were individually on our way out. This left a very large, complex project as an orphan. Nobody stepped up to lead and the project wandered in the wilderness for a few years and then died. Opportunity missed, large sums of money lost, and change was the killer.

Why didn't other executives step in to lead?

Good question. Human nature, maybe. This was a very big and risky initiative. Everyone still left standing in the company was probably just thankful to be there. The new president hadn't expressed any interest in the project. Why would they? I don't blame them. I do think the corporate CIO should have stepped up, not to lead the project but to call out the question: Hey, we got this $50 million train pulling out of the station and all our engineers are gone. Should we stop it? Postpone it? Assign it? Any solution would have been better than just letting it roll. But who knows, maybe he did, got shot down, and things just happened.

Another story of change and not being prepared was the sale of a consulting company I was with, Adjoined Consulting. Adjoined had been founded as a means to create equity, i.e. to be sold. So it was no surprise when that day came around. The sale was to a company called Kanbay out of Chicago. Kanbay had a large India-based staff that provided

IT support to financial services firms. Adjoined had a large US staff and very little financial services work. Kanbay's objective was to have the bigger US footprint drive more business back to India. This worked out okay. We each kept doing what we did and Adjoined would as appropriate throw some business to the Indian side of the house. Everything was cool.

What wasn't quite as cool was that within nine months, Kanbay sold itself to Capgemini, a global consultancy with tens of thousands of employees around the world. Capgemini was based out of Paris and had a substantial US presence that essentially already did what we did. They were not going to let us just go our own way.

A sign of the level of change to come was when they quickly took away all our laptops and reissued us new ones. It wasn't because there was anything wrong with ours, we all had practically new Lenovos, it was just that they weren't Capgemini's standard. The second thing was they had certain standard business terms that they wanted in every client contract, even active contracts. This required some discussion, but we got it done.

One of my clients did balk, but they were willing to work with us and provided alternative language. The New York office, which was HQ for the US, was unwilling to consider it and told me anything like that would have to go through Paris. They said that in hushed, awed tones as if no one would ever dream of asking the Paris office for something. Well, I was stupid and called Paris. The legal counsel I spoke to was very reasonable, read over the proposed language and agreed to it. Problem solved.

The last change that hit us though was one that really wasn't easily addressed. In the consulting business, or any services business for that matter, you tend to set your billing rates as some function of your labor costs. Some do it as a gross margin calculation, others apply some formula to gross up labor costs to include overheads, payroll taxes, benefits, etc. However it's done, it starts with labor cost. We and Capgemini both did it the same way, but the problem was their average labor cost for each employee level was dramatically higher than ours. When they started calculating project profitability using their costing models, all our projects went from big money makers to big money losers, at least in theory. In fact, nobody had gotten a raise so real margin was still the same. But they didn't care about that; they did everything on a standard costing basis.

In retrospect we should have been more careful about how we titled people when we transferred everyone in to the new organization. We just brought everyone over with the title they had. If you were a VP in Kanbay/Adjoined you were a VP in Capgemini. Same for directors, managers, senior consultants, etc.

This misalignment of costs caused a great deal of stress. I found the only thing I could do was to dramatically drop my billable hours and use that money to try and offset other shortfalls. I knew this was only a short-term solution because I was expected to have billable hours. Unfortunately I was in the outsourcing group and all our projects were long-term contracts. I couldn't work myself out of many of the deals for 8 to 10 years.

However, I also realized that even if I managed to pull a rabbit out of my hat, I didn't like what I saw my role evolving to. Instead of being an entrepreneur who found and negotiated deals and then worked closely with clients, I was going to have to be a pimp with a stable of staff to move. I had no interest in that, so I rejoined the consulting firm I had founded some eight years earlier and resumed doing what I loved.

The point of the Kanbay/Capgemini change story is that even though we intuitively knew the Capgemini deal would bring change, we didn't think it through and were thus not able to prevent some fallout. By keeping my eye on the goal of customer service I was able to adapt to some change, the contract requirements, but I could not adapt to the costing issue. For that change I had two choices. Every month I could go once more into the trenches and try to explain the true financial picture of each account or I could change my situation. Given that even without the costing problem I didn't like the look of the new situation, I chose to leave.

If your actual cost was lower than their average cost, why couldn't they use those costs when evaluating projects?

They had one policy, one way of doing things. We were insignificant to them. They had bought the company for the Kanbay part, not Adjoined. The sooner they could be rid of us the better. We certainly weren't worth changing processes for.

That's just speculation, you don't know that?

Ah, but I do. Just after I left Capgemini, a group specializing in PeopleSoft HR systems that Adjoined had bought just before selling out to Kanbay approached Capgemini about being let out of their noncompete agreements. They wanted to go back to just focusing on those types of projects for the margins they were used to making. Not only did Capgemini release them from their noncompete obligations, they gave them the clients and ongoing projects in that area, effectively giving these guys back the business Adjoined had bought from them two years prior. Really great guys. It goes to show that sometimes good things do happen to nice people. But, it also shows without question they had no interest in the business Adjoined had. It would either be forced into Capgemini's model or let go. Also a damn good demonstration of Ask and Ye Shall Receive.

The last story of change and the unexpected impacts it can have is when we sold Clinical to the private equity firm. Throughout the tire-kicking and courtship phase we had been assured that it would still be our company to run. They would provide whatever advice we might ask for and any support we needed. That sounded good to us, and since none of the private equity principals had a clue what our business was, seemed very practical as well.

What we missed, however, was that these were numbers guys. They understood financial statements and financial markets. Their primary focus was solely on the numbers. Once the wedding was over, the first thing they wanted to do was to establish a monthly, later weekly, phone call to go over some high-level metrics.

On the surface this request seemed highly reasonable. They did own about 70% of the business so had every right to want to have insight. However, there were two downsides: 1) they developed metrics we'd never used so there was some confusion on our part about what we were reporting and 2) our culture was not to do any meeting without a fully scripted, vetted and practiced deck. These simple monthly calls began to require more and more time from the chairman, head of operations, and head of sales, taking them away from doing anything operational as they focused on crafting the reports and discussion decks to put a positive spin on whatever the metrics were saying. As the metrics started to say bad things, the time spent on preparing for meetings, including quarterly board meetings, became all consuming.

With our chairman, Boris, not focused on helping sales or operations, things started to spiral. Although I honestly can't say if the head of ops and head of sales being absent from their operational duties hurt, Boris being consumed by it *did* hurt.

In this story of change, it wasn't the change itself that caused the trouble -- we knew it was coming, it was our reaction to it that caused issues. We didn't keep our eye on the goal of selling new work and servicing sponsors. We got consumed with trying to explain, train, and convince the new ownership group. In retrospect, I think they would have accepted it if we'd just said leave us the hell alone, we've got business to sell, then gone out and sold it. But, we tried to do both, with most of the focus shifting internally.

In conclusion:

a. Circumstances and people change, so you must expect to have to adjust.

b. Maintain focus on the goal and plot a new course.

c. Sometimes a strategic retreat is better than once more into the trenches.

Conversation 15 – Useful Hints

As I wrote this book, I found a few points that just didn't seem to fit neatly into the 14 original conversations. Rather than leave them out, I decided to put them here. They may not have the same level of backing experience as the first 14 do, but I have found they usually are true and useful guideposts to have.

1. Gary's Law of Constant Numbers

Simply put, no matter how many times you estimate something, you always come up with roughly the same answer.

Now, there's logic to this. When you do an estimate you include facts (those don't change between runs), assumptions and values for those assumptions (those do change). The problem is that in spite of your best efforts, if you keep running the estimator yourself, you're generally going to keep getting a similar answer. Why? Because you just can't avoid letting your bias slip in. You might change the value for one assumption and then change another with the net effect being the two changes cancel each other out. Or, you might come up with some new assumptions which turn out to be just new names for the old ones. I've done this too many times to count. You calculate and recalculate and recalculate again and you keep coming up with essentially the same answer. Time wasted. Should have trusted yourself.

If you truly want to get another estimate, have somebody else do it. Otherwise you're just killing time circling the same point.

2. Work will expand to meet the time allocated to it

On this one I have actual hard data. While at Ryder I would get a report every week from IBM on our CPU usage. The weeks were very predictable. Higher usage on Mondays trickling down as we moved to Friday. Even if there was a holiday or even an unexpected day off (hurricane) the trend was the same – Mondays high, Fridays low. If a day was missed, planned or not, you didn't see that work appear before or after in the data. It was just never done. It was as if maybe it was never needed. Thus, my hypothesis.

3. If asked to change, people will resist. If told to change, people will grumble but comply. If change just happens, people will peacefully carry on.

Change, big or small, positive or negative, is hard to push through an enterprise. The more you talk about change sometimes it seems the more resistance you get. And the more you try to bring people into the process, it seems that resistance just turns to stone and won't be moved. On the other hand if you compel change, it will happen, but everyone will complain, whine and blame the change for every issue including the weather. However, if change just occurs, people will quietly go about their work as if nothing happened.

Given the three options, if you don't have the option of making change happen without anyone noticing, I recommend commanding it.

I know that's contrary to all the teaching on change management. Remember though, a lot of people make a lot of money on pushing change management programs. And, it all sounds so good, buy-in and all that stuff. But, when it comes to hard change, well, that's what management gets paid for. Just do it!

4. Company culture is hard to define and even harder to change

I don't think anyone can tell you exactly where a company's culture came from. It just seems to evolve. It also doesn't always reflect what the marketing and executive teams say it is. To find out the true culture, you have to listen with all your senses.

Once a culture is in place, it becomes an immovable object and irresistible force all in one. Short of massive turnover of people and significant new leadership, it can't be changed. As an employee, even a senior one, all you can do is adapt or find a culture that fits you better.

5. You can mitigate risk but you cannot eliminate risk.

This one is probably self-explanatory. Any endeavor, small or large, involves some element of risk. With prudent planning and contingencies, you can mitigate the risk and make it acceptable to proceed. However, you can never eliminate risk.

Elimination will always prove too costly, every time. And, if you think you can eliminate risk by just not doing something, re-read Conversation 2. You've got to move to survive.

6. **There are lies, damn lies, and then statistics. The corollary: Figures lie and liars figure.**

Now this one is not original to me, but I am a big believer. The issue is not that the numbers themselves lie, it's how they are being interpreted that you have to watch out for. This is particularly true with percentages. If you don't know the size of the sample, any analysis based solely on percentages can be very misleading. To illustrate, one favorite of businesses is to quote growth in terms of percentages. While on the surface that might make some sense, it gets misleading as you approach either end of the business size spectrum. For a business making $1000 to go to $2000 is a 100% growth rate, while one that went from $100,000 to $125,000 is only growing at 25 percent. But who's doing better? The guy who added $25K to his bottom line.

Epilogue

Now we come to the end, or maybe it's just the midpoint. Whichever it is, I hope that you enjoyed my musings and found something of value that you can use in your business career now and in the future. Writing this has been a pleasure, allowing me to reminisce and smile at some of the events that happened over the years and the friends and associates who came into my life and left during that time.

Writing is also harder than it looks. I applaud the professional authors who have the skill to do this for a living. Telling a story with no visual or verbal clues as to whether you're getting through to your audience is very disconcerting.

As I leave you, I want to wish you the very best for success and enjoyment in your chosen career. As the Irish say, "May the road rise up to meet you, and may you always have the wind at your back."

Cheers!

Gary

About the Author

Gary Urban is a senior business executive with the proven ability to provide strong leadership and strategic thinking across multiple industries and businesses. Continual learning for himself and the developmental coaching of others has always been one of his core passions. With more than 40 years' experience with global consultancies Accenture and CapGemini, Fortune 500 companies such as Ryder System, start-ups with a successful equity transaction exits (Adjoined and Biorasi), and having started two businesses of his own (UPi Urban Partners and Logan Studios), Gary has a wealth of hands-on information, ideas, and knowledge to pass on.

Gary holds a BSBA in Economics and an MBA in Finance, both from the University of Florida. He also has an honorary Doctor of Divinity degree from Universal Life Church. He is certified in Good Clinical Practices (GCP) and COVID-19 Business Compliance.

Currently he is the Managing Partner at UPi (Urban Partners, Inc.), a consultancy he founded more than 20 years ago. He also serves on the board of directors at several other companies.

    He is available for interviews and speaking engagements. He can be contacted through UPi at www.upiurbanpartners.com

www.ingramcontent.com/pod-product-compliance
Lightning Source LLC
Chambersburg PA
CBHW072030230526
45466CB00020B/1219